First published in the UK 2022 by Sizewise Studio Limited
Cover design by sizewisestudio.com

© Joe Winter 2022

Joe Winter has asserted his right under the Copyright, Designs and Patents Act, 1988, to be identified as the author of this work.
ISBN number: 978-1-7397450-1-1

All rights reserved. No part of this publication may be reproduced, stored in a retrieval sytem, or transmitted, in any form or by any means, electronic, mechanical, photocopying, recording or otherwise, without the prior permission of the copyright holder.

A catalogue record for this book is available from the British Library.

A Word in Your Shell-like

Contents

Introduction 2
What're they doing to my tree? 4
Two worlds. 6
Keon Lincoln 8
It's breathing 10
Asphodel Long 12
What is it with this crazy 'soap'? 14
Books 16
Ballad of the Socks 18
50 Snapping Turtles 20
In Time of Covid 22
ROOOT! 24
Dreams 26
Forget about God 28
House of Cards 30
Fattypuffs and Thinifers 32
Seasoning 34
Harry. 36
Meghan 38
Storm. 40
People, people everywhere 42
The lights of day appeared 44
Just a stone 46
Day of Reflection 48
The Flower Stand 50
Sooner or later. 52

Dirge against the Dons	54
Let bishops fianchetto	56
Shiva	58
Shiva	60
Mrs Tinckham and Mrs Canuticacq	62
Prince Philip	64
Peace	66
War	68
Shirley Williams	70
Surviving the Death Railway	72
Warhol Immersive	74
Jimmy White and world peace	76
Words	78
Roads	80
Clouds	82
Winds	84
E.B.B.	86
Saraswati	88
The Satanic Verses	90
The Satanic Verses	92
Election Special	94
Is it even worth saying?	96
The Spectator	98
The living stream	100
Ballad to the Pubs' Re-opening	102
Those dancing chips	104

Contents *continued*

George Street	106
Manchester United	108
The train set in the attic	110
Leaf burst	112
Techers	114
Techers	116
Tantum religio	118
A Wild Flower	120
Unholy places	122
Uncle Simek	124
Somewhere beyond a threshold	126
Little Gidding	128
Whiff-whaff	130
The first days	132
Halo-virus	134
Busker	136
The ball-game	138
Rabindranath	140
Rabindranath	142
Rabindranath	144
Tagore and Gandhi	146
Tagore and Gandhi	148
Ballad of the Tins	150
It's Italy on penalties	152
On the run	154
Freedom Day	156

A Rubbish Heap	158
Pet-Hates on Nightingales	160
Time	162
The Olympic Flame	164
S.W.A.T.	166
At the Clifto	168
At Lagwyne Cottage	170
At Lagwyne Cottage	172
Old and new	174
Durga	176
A new game	178
Ballad of the Books	180
If we are free	182
In Ashdown Forest	184
The human dimension	186
Kali	188
Kali	190
Chas.	192
The Power and the Glory	194
The ad fad	196
A vote of thanks	198
Mare noctis	200
Finale	202

Introduction

In January 2021, stymied as a poet by a writer's block (the first in my life), I decided to try out a different approach. I would write a blog on a newly set-up website (joewinter-poet.com). This quickly turned into as creative a venture as any of my poems. I know this from the claims it made on me, by occupying my thinking and non-thinking life alike, simply as a presence. "Feed the rat," say mountaineers. This rat sat expectant, or actively chewed away at my mind, often occasioning a bedside lamp to be switched on and off half the night for a thought to be followed up or recast, ventured or abandoned. But all the time I viewed it not as the writing of a poem but as something more ephemeral in the sense of day-to-day; and if an entry was to last (in the literal sense of ephemeral) for one day only, so be it. This collection is published in the hope that overall at least it may be worth a few days more.

From January to September a new topic would bounce out at me every few days. Some took more than one entry to deal with, or to deal with me. Certain themes emerged. The Covid "freeze" and emergence from lockdown; the power of women (this from the probably unique standpoint of poetry written in the classrooms of London comprehensives, together with a kind of personal brush with the Hindu female deity); and the occasional reflection on conflict resolution near and far. It all sounds deadly serious. In fact it's a lighthearted response to the times and to my own time, with the trivial outweighing the weighty by a fair few pages; and since finishing its century of entries (which seemed a good place to stop) I've started writing poetry again. Some may find a touch within. It's been a riot to write and I hope there'll be something for everybody who finds the time to leaf through it.

The Brothers, a poem of an elm-tree (and myself) outside my window that the first and last entries refer to, can be found on my website (see above).

I would like to thank my son Chris Winter for his amazing work in setting up the website, in transferring not only all my poetry to it but specifically this blog as it came out, and for sorting out the pictures for the various entries. He coped with my finickiness with remarkable patience and craftsmanship. I would also like to thank certain friends and other members of the family who took an interest in this or that entry; and to wish readers well.

What're they doing to my tree?
January 22nd 2021

Of course it's not my tree, I half-apologise to it as I raise the blinds at an infernal noise in the street and see two men assailing its twiggy lower branches. Well, not really branches at all but the wispy trunk-fluff beneath the branches proper. The noise is from a truck where similar shavings from trees down the road are being shredded into dust and blasted into a heap on the truck floor. My outrage melts away as I see the lower trunk look trimmer and fitter as the men move on, and I give a light nod through the window to my old friend, waiting patiently in the winter sunlight for the garb of Spring.

For a start, it's the road's tree, or rather the pavement's: it just happens to stand outside my first-floor flat from which I'm often aware of its life-affirming outstretch, an amazing twist of torso-and-arms that begins on a level with my eyes. Two years ago as the leaves returned we had a conversation that did wonders for me at a slightly lowish time. I recorded it in *The Brothers* (see Introduction), and it's that privilege of kinship that also makes me rue calling this old elm "mine".

In the poetic world where the conversation took place it was hardly even an elm or I a human, we were neighbours in Nature and for a moment it seemed, close family. I say "old" but it's probably within 25 years or so of my age, round about its century now and going strong.

Again I admire its well-shaven trunk as I turn back to ordinary life and wonder when the barber's going to re-open, lightly touching the side of my neck.

Two worlds

January 26th 2021

I can't help thinking about two worlds. One in which we take an imaginative step forward in some needy area of social life – immigration, say, or education – and the other where we continue to grind out an immeasurably slow pace of change that may or may not deliver any positive result at all. It probably does, on the whole, in the very long run, at unbelievable expense. It seems to be the practical way to go about things, however frustratingly unwieldy, backsliding and slow. But if only we could allow the impractical, imaginative side a touch more into our thinking, into our dreams!

Take immigration (disregarding the present Covid restriction). Most people have a fairly clear idea of what they think. I'm all over the place. On the one hand I'm delighted by the change in the nation's make-up since my childhood and say, "Yes, Britain's become a part of the world, now we have to let things develop far more slowly for the following reasons (blah blah blah), despite (blah blah blah) and additionally because (bl. bl. bl.)". On the other hand, motivated by several years of living and working in India and also by travels in Africa, I'm quietly yelling, "Open the gates! Open the gates! They have so much to teach us!"

Or take education. As a secondary-school teacher forever irked by an exam structure addicted to change I nevertheless say, "Yes, GCSEs, A

Levels, the structure they provide, the opportunity for students to set goals and go for them, bl. bl. bl., it's magnificent." At the same time I'm screaming, "So we murder creativity in children for the sake of a piece of paper. Simply ditch the whole dreary framework! Teach the subjects with just as much care for accuracy but allowing, even at times encouraging students to take the wrong path. See what they come up with!" It's a fact that in my early years of teaching English the poetry written by schoolchildren in front of my eyes was extraordinary. Then I became more part of the system.

Just two examples where I don't know what I think. Or rather I do, but I accept the collision of the two worlds inside me. Everybody has them, the incompatible pair, the practical and the ideal, the revolutionary and the staid. It's just a thought, but maybe far too many are locked into the dogma of consistency a touch more than need be, a self-contradictory position is taken as somehow "wrong" … and the revolutionary is slowly but surely, as the years go by, lowered overboard and let drift. But isn't that voice needed, in the internal discussion, to liven things up?

Or am I just being an impractical poet?

Keon Lincoln

January 27th 2021

A howl, a scream
unheard, unvoiced
unutterably savage
singes the mind's edge
outside the sky
hears nothing except
the normal click-clack
of everyday life
sees nothing unusual
inside an inferno
runs riot in flame
huddles up with the wind
I am half mad, helpless
a fifteen-year-old child
is shot and stabbed

by other children
I shall always see
his mother's sad face
and his twin sister's
just another death
carried out in broad daylight
I am shocked, but only
a small part of me
lets the shock be felt
deep, safe inside
outside the sky
hears nothing except
the normal click-clack
of everyday life
sees nothing unusual

It's breathing

January 30th 2021

It's breathing, I murmur, as I try to express the sense of oneness with atmosphere and place that seems almost to animate the ship-long building opposite me. It's a school, set up in 1884 as a blue plaque tells us, and the faded stonework inscription over the entrance suggests a community of classrooms for widely different ages, Connaught Road Council Schools. Such is the size of the whole one imagines the entire age-range at the time pouring in, pouring out. Now it doubles as an infants' school and adult education centre, only the first in action at the present time and that only partially. How good it will be to see the school-going generation out on its daily ways again, once the blight in the air is seen off!

But as one looks at the calm and capable façade opposite, it's hard to believe the good old norms won't re-assert themselves soon. With a pink restored-stone motif offsetting the brickwork and lightly containing the long narrow windows, it's at once authoritative and welcoming; formal but with a hint of warmth; anything but severe. It settles into the surround – and how much that must have changed over the time – with a quite wonderful composure. The blue plaque commemorates the architect, one Thomas Simpson, who seems to have combined something of the imposing Queen Anne style with a utilitarian outlook, so that all has its place. A quiet and unobtrusive harmony is at one with the road.

With the changing weather and light it constantly takes one by surprise, especially for me when the sunlight suddenly illuminates the brickwork. In these strange times I've found it a symbol of reassurance and hope, of life that will soon return in a good air, when we are more at ease again. Perhaps far and wide, when we can breathe more freely, we can be a little more on good terms with the environment, as this old building seems to be now.

Asphodel Long

February 1ˢᵗ 2021

Sixteen years ago she passed away. Just the other day I was talking to my brother on the phone, her other child. She had no daughters. And yet she did, a bevy of them far and near, younger women for whom, behind the scenes, I think she offered a mother's touch. I hadn't realised this until this moment of writing. She was a good friend to any number of people, women and men of any age, and naturally to children. She may have been a mother-figure in a way to some of the men as well. But looking back I see she was able to give something especially to younger women. Perhaps beyond her ability to listen and understand it was an alliance, a matter of simply being there in a shared concern. It was a gift the more telling in that she had not known any kind of a mother herself.

It is a mark of her bravery that she turned something bad into something good. She had had an exceptionally turbulent and traumatic childhood and launched out on her own into an independent young adulthood which led to a somewhat rocky road. She made it work. She earned a living as a textiles journalist and in her middle age, her two sons grown, plunged into the burgeoning women's movement and became a well-known figure in it, especially towards the end of her life. Her book 'In a Chariot Drawn by Lions' was and is used widely as a resource by those who wish to explore the historical figure of Wisdom as the female aspect of divinity. She published a store of articles in the same broad area. Her life had expanded: yet she was never the kind of scholar who got in the way of who she really was. She had always been a practical person. She had also always been a poet.

Her other published book, a volume of poetry called 'Athene Revisited' and dedicated *to the furies*, is less known and deserves to be more so. I have been reading it on and off all day. There's a poem, 'Full Moon in Malta', which after seeing the moon as boat at night and globe fruit at dawn bursting into sunlight, plunges into the darkness of the doubt of day, with so much subject to 'human despoilers'. Finally the day, too, takes her by surprise:

As I walked the grey road in the afternoon dusk
Seeing a patchy field, where wild daisies danced in thorns and stones
And a group of goats backed down to harbour,
In the green folds of the thin grass
Suddenly, another fruit, another boat, another pattern,
Suddenly whole groups, among the grass and the thistles and the wild clover
Suddenly in the singing evening, as the first star climbed upwards
Suddenly in the dusty road, bending mildly towards me
In the damp evening,
Suddenly I saw, looked again and saw
The merciful corn.

My mother lifted people. She was a part of the undying world of clarity and common-sense and hope – and vision. She had tremendous strength. She was a great soul. My brother and I have not always seen eye to eye but in our different ways we are glad of what she gave us, and know we are more than privileged. The next time we chat on the phone – we're in different countries – I dare say some recognition of that will pass between us, a flicker of that flame. Though always far more is unsaid than said, it usually does.

What is it with this crazy 'soap'?

February 9th 2021

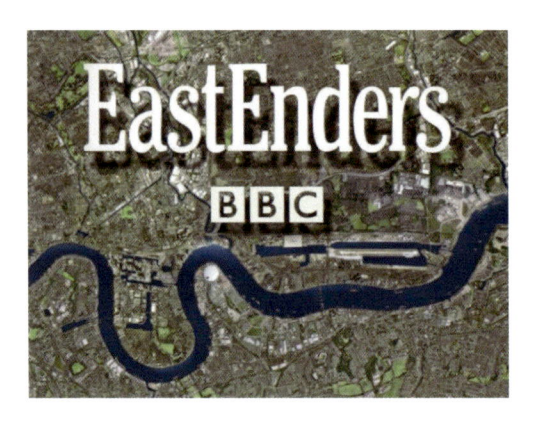

I saw what I believe was the first episode of 'EastEnders', way back in the dark ages, and remember nothing of its plot or characters; but an underlying feature stayed with me. In a café, in a pub, at a market stall people were scratching a living as they talked; a bustle of work drew me in; and soon enough I was caught up in their shenanigans. A wild ball of thread spun round Albert Square, looping round this character, discarding that, unravelling in terms of probability as fast as it gathered in melodramatic stature, as a medley of lives hurtled on their way. Yet the pace of events had its slow side, too. Some of the most memorable episodes have been a two-hander, or even a single character musing, talking aloud for the witching half-hour. The series invited me onto an island of the absurd, and I went back to it again and again, for despite the ever-entangling plot-lines something has always carried its own conviction. Beneath the nonsense there winds a binding-thread of the everyday. A sense of reality permeates the circus of events; decisions are taken for good and bad; and unexpected moments of insight and humanity are on offer far more often than its detractors who sometimes call it 'DeadEnders' care to believe. I have watched it, on and off, for nigh on half my life.

The acting has been superb. The photography too; almost with every episode there are presentational techniques to admire for their own sake.

Certain actors stay in the part and age with it; others leave and within days we accept a new and different acting talent in an old role, an old acquaintance almost; and watch with awe as they re-shape the character to their strengths, and as we ourselves subtly co-operate by half-abandoning memories that don't fit. Some actors cannot be replaced: Dot Cotton, Phil Mitchell live and die with their "handlers", June Brown and Steve McFadden, who for my money should be damed and knighted forthwith. The substance of the roles may be less than Shakespearean; but the performance has been epic. And as I say, the unexpected moments, in this character and that, and over the series as a whole, give it its depth: the programme can touch upon the abiding questions, the island of the absurd can be not a million miles away from our world. And always on the simple level of entertainment – it's a riot.

It is art; but art cannot be made of this. I have written poems about paintings, about films; but I am less likely to write a poem about the Queen Vic than I am to down a pint in it. Even so I raise a glass to it as I write. To a crazy and magnificent sequence – to a sequence of no consequence – long may it roll!

Books

February 12th 2021

It's 1967, my first teaching post. I'm covering for an absent English teacher at a girls' comprehensive school in Islington, London for the summer term. After a bewildering and personally very difficult year or two post-university including a number of very short-term jobs I've managed to find something I think I may want to do. I've no idea how to manage recalcitrant individuals or whole classes when they get "lairy", and they can spot my hesitancy. Children in groups are psychological instruments of great accuracy and merciless intent. I had had no teacher training – in those days it wasn't an absolute requirement, one learnt on the job – and indeed I've always been glad that was how I started.

Anyhow, to the issue on hand: a miracle happened in my first few years in the classroom. Despite any number of disciplinary problems I also had some success, but there was one area in which success is simply the wrong word. I was witness to, and indeed helped to bring about, a river of jewels, a cascade of poems written by children, mostly sitting in front of me in the classroom itself, that has refreshed my entire life since. From time to time in this blog I'll mention one of these poets and poems. This was from one of the very youngest, a girl of 11 or 12 years old called Jacqueline Campbell.

BOOKS

Lined up, Straight backed,
Corporal dictionary,
Lieutenants that's the fiction books,
Quick Quick straight backs,
All in a row
Stand the books.

It's a kind of proto-poetry that deals in the very essence of the alchemy of art. The moving world joins forces with the still. The reader's mind is opened, a play is enacted, the curtain is drawn. The image is alive. To say any more is to interfere with the adventure of her statement and I may already have said too much. I didn't even teach Jacqueline – I had been asked to take a library lesson, where the children read a book quietly, as a brief swap in the timetable – and she handed me this. Later her form mistress gave me a few more she'd written but for some reason I didn't get round to seeing her again and then the term was over and I left the school.

Later there were to be many more, from older children at other schools; but these priceless sheets of paper gradually dried up after a few years. I became too distant from the pupils, perhaps, in terms of age; I was more preoccupied with running a department; or simply, the precarious position I was in when I joined that first school had more or less evaporated: I had grown up. But as a welcoming-gift to a profession that snow-drift of paper sheets, with its glittering array of words, can rarely have been equalled.

Ballad of the Socks
February 13th 2021

Socks – they come in twos,
   or so the story goes,
but mine have different views.
   It's as if one chose
the right of a recluse
   to freedom, and won't share it
in ways that others use.
   Each sock is a free spirit.

But while one sock pursues
   a lonely life, stays single
in the wrong drawer, to lose
   itself, and its twin Pringle . . .
another leaves long queues
   of the mismatched. I wear it –
to later learn the old news.
   Each sock is a free spirit.

These fellows who abuse
  the standards of society,
who skulk alone, or choose
  in colourful impropriety
each other to amuse . . .
  we have to grin and bear it,
and celebrate their hues.
  Each sock is a free spirit.

Reader, I say, excuse
  the darn lot. Or I swear it,
I wouldn't be in your shoes.
  Each sock is a free spirit.

50 Snapping Turtles
February 18th 2021

Three weeks ago it was over but the memory can still flare up of a protracted, nightmarish encounter. My elder son and I are intrinsically competitive and when we take each other on, with the best spirit in the world, it can be tough going. He's recently taken over as *numero uno* in table-tennis, after a long spell (merely his lifetime) of domination on my part. Before lockdown we would often meet in a pub for breakfast and a two-or-three-hour session on the Times puzzles: Quintagram, Sudoku, KenKen, Concise Crossword, Polygon and the Daily Quiz, interlaced with Brexit chat and generally setting the world to rights. Occasionally on a Sunday we'd take on the Sunday Times Jumbo GK. And then, with lockdown upon us, he threw down the gauntlet of gauntlets, or at least pushed it through my door: a book of fifty of the same.

So began a marathon of marathons. Over the next six weeks or so we did the lot, going over each one by phone. We worked out the rules as we went, for example that with a person's name of more than one word you get half a point for half the full answer, a third for a third . . . you can imagine the legalistic niceties in other instances. Which I may say we enjoyed grinding out in a kind of detailed constitutional discussion. What was bewildering was how close we were in the results.

With fifty to sixty clues in each grid incredibly we drew the first two, and ended up with the boy (in his fifties) the victor by two puzzles overall. Each of us suffered agonies over words at the back of the mind (of course we looked up nothing while solving); each of us made inspired guesses or had infuriating mind-freezes. I still can't believe I didn't get Amontillado having had it to hand as a tipple virtually for ever. He was hot on what I grouchily referred to as the bandwagon of popular music and film, I was the more likely to dig out a classical or literary reference; but either would on occasion triumph with a lucky guess in the other's area, where the "expert" had a blank space. And still a jumble of miniature successes and failures crashes through the mind, if one lets it, and one thinks: never again.

In the pictured puzzle I was relieved to get Crepe Suzette and Quiche Lorraine, as he generally runs away with the foods. I was convinced of Ambrose Pierce, forgetting it was Bierce: only a half. He put together Halicarnassus – my area, and I was stumped! – and hovering between emplane and enplane he reasoned aright and I wrong (as soon as I knew the n was wrong, of course, I couldn't believe I'd gone for it). American Pie drove me mad: I kept running the tune of the sung name through my head but was looking for a three-syllable first word and ended up only with Pie, scoring zilch. Elsewhere though I was more on song and won this particular one overall. Now, recovering GK-Jumbo-holics both, we are limited to a single puzzle when it comes out on Sunday each week. We give ourselves only an hour (with the book we had unlimited time for each for a day or so). We discuss the results by phone and that's it. Each is trying to forget the compulsive agony of the binge of the past. Never again.

Except that the other day he shoved another collection of the same through the door, 50 more snapping turtles. The internet says these animals may attack if humans interact with them. Neither of us can look the first one in the eye yet – but we know a six-weeks bender's on its way. We're in for a mauling – it's my turn to win – bring it on!

In Time of Covid

February 21st 2021

As many millions will have done and many more will do, I need to jot down a thought or two on the bane of the time. It's a shock on the face of the globe; the world is stopped in its tracks. The suffering and death of so many, especially among the old and the disabled, is a horror of horrors, a nail through the heart. The enforced loneliness of so many individuals, the disruption to so many families, the unimaginable strains on so many denied assistance, the check in social and educational development, like a spoke in the wheel, to the world's cohort of children – it has all cut too deep to see. Economically it is a debilitating blow to the global system, but the economic recovery will be quicker than the human one. There is a long way to come back.

But there is an upside, if it's only an opportunity. It is unlikely, and yet just about imaginable, that we can return to a marginally better place than we were in before. Over time – and it will take a long time – there can be a healing process with an added degree of fortification. A restorative ingredient is available to us and already at work that can act against the deadly danger not of Covid – but of non-co-operation.

Virtually every country has been on the receiving end of this savagery of Nature. Human responsibility for the catastrophe has been at worst no more than carelessness. We can feel – and already do – a single people, injured by a common marauder. And to an infinitely greater extent than, say, in the (far more catastrophic) Black Death, or after the abattoir of the Second World War, we have the means at hand to interconnect more as one people, and so to make ourselves more whole.

We are now an interlinked world with communication to all parts of the system increasing at an exponential rate. Yes, the geopolitical rivalries and anxieties that clutter the globe are not going to go away. But to recover from the shock of Covid it is not impossible that a health-giving factor within the new technology will come more into play. To put it at its simplest – the ability we now have to link up stands more of a chance of being used to our well-being. For a time at least we will be a touch more aware of our shared needs. Vaccine-sharing is the first indication of this happening. Likely enough it'll all go back to more of the same. And yet – who knows? History may yet record the very faintest of lifts in the long long trek of the species to a decently co-operative state of affairs.

It's a trite enough thought, I know. But I needed to clear my head.

ROOOT!
February 23rd 2021

The deep cry echoes out from the terraces. Joe Root deftly guides another four behind the wicket. He's closing in on his century. ROOOT!

Empty terraces here these days. But I can imagine midweek, up and down England, the air shaking in sitting-rooms to the cry. It's one-all against India in a four-Test series – in India. If by some miracle we can win the final two games at Ahmedabad, possibly on a lusher, more predictable wicket than the Chennai jack-in-the-box now behind us, we'll make the final of the ICC World Test Championship. But to win a series so decisively in India is like – well, me hitting a six onto the shed roof in a 3rd XI match at school back in 1961. But it happened.

The final's slated to be played at Lord's in June. I saw Root bat there in 2013 against the Australians. Not only did he make 180, his slow spin took two wickets for nine runs. I've always rated him as a bowler and wish now as captain he'd put himself on more. It may sound as if I think he's the bee's knees. Not so at all.

For four years – ever since he took up the captaincy – I've been snarling at the screen. With plenty of others I've felt the responsibility's got in the way of his quite exceptional batting talent. I've also felt he isn't a natural captain anyway. Too nice, with that infuriating shy smile at the crease when he should be stony-faced, standing tall, dominating the surround. Young for his years and too young anyway. How can he be anyone's boss? Let alone – ! Something thoroughly nasty in me has wanted to yell out, Give him the BOOOT!

Sport's a wonderful, terrible thing. In fact his captaincy record is an excellent one. And lately he's been knocking out double centuries as well as leading the team on an outstanding run. Sport can make animals out of us. I shall never forget being on a train in Glasgow as it crawled past a train crawling the other way. Mine was filled with Celtic supporters, the other with Rangers. A mass of vicious, snarling faces on each side spat from the windows at their opposite numbers, hands turned to claws . . . then the other train was out of sight and life returned to normal. Sport doesn't need this. Joe Root's unassuming, balanced approach has in fact turned out very well. May he have many more years at the helm.

And may he bat like an angel (an angel couldn't but I'm sure he can) in the forthcoming deciders. Roll on midweek. And let's hope the terraces will be allowed to fill again later in the year, and that deep cry again roll out over the field at boundary after boundary.

ROOOT!!

Dreams
February 26th 2021

Dreams. What are they for? A digestive process of the mind, as it seems, often including a conscious "chewing-over" of some part or other the next day or days. But what one can remember of the detail can be altogether bewitching and extraordinary. What kind of troglodytic artist is it in the cave of the skull that can sketch out a vignette with such attention to the minutiae of scene and story? Plot, colour, a kaleidoscopic journey on an ever-changing stage, a steady focus on the refinement of one's inner feeling . . . and yet one's asleep. Nothing's ever quite tied up, nothing's ever determined . . . except as it may be at a completely buried level. The strange cinematic adventure is not confined to humans, it would seem. Other animals too appear to experience some echo of the hunt and play of the waking round, in the unconscious artform of dream.

So much of what goes on in the brain is a mystery. And so one trusts it will remain: so that whatever further progress is made on the identity map, we will never find ourselves at the end. Meanwhile a certain strangeness is a part of the everyday, or everynight; and sometimes, unexpectedly, that is where we can in truth find ourselves.

THE LADY

Innocently she stands,
Quietly she stands.
Now she fades,
Walking through the hall.
All that see
Whisper the tales
They've heard.

This is another poem by Jacqueline Campbell (see page 16), a preteen at home in an equipoise of the opposites. Is her lady ghost or real, substantial or dream? But then – what is dream?

Maybe it is the pre-artist at work, a back-turn of the page from conscious thought, an evolutionary gate to the broader expanse of the human. Then before they catch us up – must machines learn to dream?

Forget about God
March 2nd 2021

. . . and find a new story. A story that can appeal to the child in us, but that looks more to the future than the past. We don't need a creation myth, now that science is regularly exploding secrets of the universe near and (comparatively) far; the one at the back of it all can wait as we look ahead. We don't need an explanation of "evil"; the idea of original sin is simply erased from the present reality; on the moral plane too we are grappling near and far with life's intricacies. We are losing interest in a post-death system that rewards good behaviour instead of leaving it as its own reward. But we do continue to need a way of being together that includes symbol, singing words and silent commitment, a place to congregate that cherishes an ideal. We need some kind of temple to the future.

Can a story be spun of a world at one, can a vision quietly take some tangible form, to give us a rail to hold on to, so to speak, at a time of breakneck development and change? Could that rail, differently formed in terms of language and other cultural material, be a link for us all to join forces, or even, as it might be, hands? I'm dreaming I know. But what brought this on was passing a couple of churches in my daily lockdown walk and wishing I could go in and sit down – as simple as that. I've always been astonished at the volume of a typically tall church, its towering empty spaces, that seem to have endless room for all the voices of the past. Such characters are there, a community down the centuries. What a concept it has been and still is, to capture and surround such a space, to breathe God's magnificence. And yet the concept is slowly but surely altering with the time.

When the churches do open again I shall go in, now and then, and listen to the voices of the present and the past, and maybe even join in the singing of a hymn or two from my childhood. And I shall wonder how things could be someday, if by some miracle we could take something fine from the past and use it for something fine in the future. It would take a narrative to form of a more practical vision, a new magnificence. But first we must learn to forget about God.

House of Cards
March 3rd 2021

Blimey. An unAmerican expression perhaps but after watching the full 73 episodes of my latest Netflix blow-out – Suits and Breaking Bad went before – I need to remind myself I wasn't, er, born in the USA. I've been riveted by all three – I'm almost grateful to lockdown that I stumbled into the genre. But the pace of it all is crazy. On my one trip to the actual region I found pretty well everyone calm and sane and even considerate; and yet there's always an underlying sense of things going too fast, somehow, a sense which may be reflected in their film. Perhaps it's not who Americans are but how they see themselves.

Frank and Claire Underwood, a married couple who become successive Presidents, hurtle through international crises and a kind of quick-change dance of cut-throat politics at home, to provide almost unforgettable portraits of what may be called survivor's power. And 'cut-throat' is hardly metaphorical. At one point during Frank's term a crowd is baying, "Blunderwood! Blunderwood!" and at every session following I bawled "Blood and Thunderward" at the television before turning it on. But I loved it all. One or two of the minor characters in particular were a treat and Doug Stamper an immortal.

But the producers missed a trick. When Frank dies and Claire is elevated from the Vice-Presidency, I was seething at how she was hectored, interrupted and patronised by all the male politicos around her. (I've long been of the view that men should be excluded from the politics of the world.) And so I was delighted when out of the blue Claire dismissed her Cabinet wholesale, appointed a new one and suddenly was at the head of a long table at which sat twenty or so women – and no man. Now – in spite of more than a sprinkling of the Lady Macbeth element – we would see a different reaction in Dr Strangelove's laboratory. By which I mean, in however nefarious a plot-line, the world of rivalries at least for a scene or two might yield up a glimpse of a new construct, where (to put it bluntly) people didn't simply talk each other down.

Not a bit of it. The producers set it up and forgot what they were after. I suppose the most exciting thing in building a house of cards is when it topples, not when it stays up, at least in filmic terms. I shall remember the series for its underlying savagery, but also for a number of moments of individual pathos, and a moving portrayal of an unusual marriage. But most of all I shall remember it for a moment that didn't happen.

Fattypuffs and Thinifers
March 5th 2021

It was my first book and I would still say it is my favourite one. An old friend of the family gave it me when I was two or three, probably just after the end of the War. And war is what it's about, war and peace, though on a somewhat less searing level than Tolstoy's epic. For me it was about the wonderful pictures of the worlds of thin people and fat people.

It's still in remarkably good shape, with its old faded green binding and all the pages in place. Written by André Maurois in 1930 (under the title 'Patapoufs et Filifers') and translated and brought out in Great Britain in 1941, it kept the original imaginative artwork by Jean Bruller, without which it's scarcely more than an adventurous yarn. But those illustrations have kept the heart of a child alive in at least one old sourpuss up and down the rollercoaster of the post-War world.

There are pictures of two brothers and their parents, mother and Edmond on the plump side, father and Terry anything but – it's all gloriously incorrect by modern standards. The boys scramble up a couple of facing rocks and drop down between them to find a moving staircase rumbling down into the Earth. At the bottom they're separated by guards and for months don't see each other, as they're made to live in two size-ist subterranean countries, in which everything's either sharp and pointed (including birds and beasts, even coastline), or rounded and somehow genially comfortable. You can't help warming to the Fattypuffs, unhurried as they are and fond of food. The picture of a typical Fattypuff bed made me vow to find one or make one like that when I grew up. (The Thinifer bed pitches you into a narrow basin of cold water at 5 a.m.)

The war's about the name of the island in the middle of the sea that parts the two countries. Is it to be Thinipuff or Fattyfer? Eventually of course the frighteningly energetic Thinifers prevail over their easygoing opponents . . . but come the peace, the warmer disposition of the losers gradually engages the others, whose eyes begin to be opened . . . so that after a time neither comes out on top nor needs to. Hybrid buildings and buses are born, strange weddings take place . . . life is shared even as visible characteristics stay distinct. Oh, and the name of the island? Someone suggests 'Peachblossom Island' and the problem's solved.

When the boys ascend the staircase, after ten months away, and scramble up between the rocks, they're amazed to see their father standing nearby and no more than a trifle impatient. The final sentence has always made excellent sense so far as I'm concerned, though I understand it as little now as when it was first read to me.

'The fact is that in the kingdoms of the Underground, where there is neither sun nor moon, time goes exactly seven thousand times faster than it does on the Surface.'

Seasoning
March 7th 2021

Someone
can be known
by her way with words.

I
scarcely know her
(we've met twice briefly).

There is an illness
which comes and goes.
There is a wellness

which is here to stay.
It goes past the body
to the human Body.

There is a book of poems.
It is of a seasoning.
And in its way

it adds a seasoning
to the whole.
I am glad to know her.

On her birthday
I say thankyou
for her words.

Harry
March 9th 2021

For me the story's about Harry. A bewildered boy in the nightmare of his mother's funeral cortège, a slightly off-kilter teenager and youth, a man who found strength in the Army's camaraderie and sacrifice, a prince who launched and led the Invictus Games . . . and now? A man who has found a certain freedom.

Of course it's an illusion, as he knows even as he enjoys it: he will always be "under the net" (if not in Iris Murdoch's sense). The eyes of the world will always be upon him. He will be blamed excessively, praised excessively, hunted and haunted by the Press. Under a tree he may loll with his lovely wife but no shade will block out the words words words of others forever dissecting and describing him, in blazing capitals shouting from the sky.

He will also be hunted and haunted by his past. Many will see a textbook case of a psychic wound re-opened. In the lurid goldfish-bowl of his family, his judgement is off: you do not stir up the dark waters of racism. You do not even tell the world your father stopped taking your calls for a time. The wavering line between public and private is lost: an interview with Oprah is not a psychiatrist's couch but in terms of confidentiality its precise opposite. He has made it harder for himself to find the necessary orientation of a public figure, in a world in which that unsteady marker is changing for each individual faster than ever before.

Simply, he is pitching too much of the present onto the burning-ground of the past. There is a risk of collateral damage; certainly he will be accused of causing the same. 'The whole world is our hospital,' said T.S.Eliot (again in a very different context). Harry, it isn't. You have become a more private individual: honour that contract, which you instigated though you may be disappointed by its final terms; and the freedom you seek, even in the world's gaze, can yet be yours. A vital, generous, independent-minded spirit has so much to give. But a balance must be found. Somehow, even in the royal frenzy about to descend upon our ears, your qualities are such I believe it will. Without rancour, without rivalry, while one brother will one day be a much-admired and much-loved King, the other will burnish what is in some ways the more difficult part of a shared legacy. To his home nation as to others he will be the People's Prince.

Meghan
March 10th 2021

I'm naturally far less acquainted with Meghan's story than Harry's. Watching Suits a few months back I did gain an inkling of the world her marriage to him had shut the door on, with the effect of a door slamming. One imagined the freewheeling after-work conversations, the ribbing, the laughs, the empathy, the support this bunch of highly-talented professionals would automatically offer each other. While the interview the other day showed only too clearly the gathering nightmarish storm of her new life, as if she had indeed entered a prison-world.

Perhaps the unfortunate element in the overall situation was the theatrical set-up of the royal family itself. Meghan stepped from one role to another. I don't think it was conscious; after all, we all have a personal narrative we play out, to ourselves if no-one else. But the level of exposure of the new part, for a time the prime spot in the Biggest Show on Earth, took her over: she sailed into it, always the princess in love – how refreshing it would have been to see her snap at Harry on television! – always thrillingly beautiful, always making a fairy-tale come true. Reserve, reserve: the greatest lesson the Queen has to offer her family.

And Meghan is of that family and at a critical point in her relations with it. If now, having had her say, she can stop saying it, and step away from the blame game for good and all – it could yet come to seem hardly more than a blip, there and gone, a passing cloud in the sky. There will be visits, the cousins will play together, a new order will gradually take over and be the norm. The danger is that the role as it has developed, as if of its own volition, will gather strength. A decision is needed.

Role-playing can be desperately real. I don't think Meghan's suicidal thoughts came from nowhere – and yes, I do think she had them. What is at the centre of this and so many tragic situations is no more or less than the blame game. We hunger for it. Questions to politicians as to celebrities foam with it. Everything is treated as an investigation into a car crash. But a car accident can be no-one's fault.

If the happy couple in the picture can say, enough is enough, let it fade, let the cloud disappear, it will do so. Despite the public baying to take sides, if they are given no encouragement the need will find a different target – the most natural lying in the field of sport, where taking sides is part of the game. The true question – and it is a hard one – may be: can the actress escape her career?

Storm
March 13th 2021

Back to 1967 and my first teaching appointment (see page 16). I took (what would now be) a Year 10 class in an all-girls' school and lit on a fifteen-year-old poet of a true power. By which I mean each poem she wrote had, in its way, the 'ornament which truth doth give', as Shakespeare has it. One way to judge poetry is to think how Shakespeare would have felt reading it. Absurd as it may sound, I think he would have been at home with the drift of Orchyd Constable's work.

I had noticed her prose writing for a searching, imaginative quality. Asked to write a ghost story she had pictured a man in an African forest. The story was full of the forest's shapes and noises, but it was permeated by the darkness. The man was afraid of the dark, because it held the unknown, He was comforted by it, for the same reason. While for 'Dreams' she described lying in bed, near sleep, and looking at the pattern-shapes on the wallpaper. She asked herself the question: are those shapes over there, on the wall, or here, in my brain? Somehow, quite simply, she suggested the beginnings of free play in the mind that is a main element of dreams.

Her writing was untidy, not a little mis-spelt, and did not reflect a background of sophisticated or "clever" ideas. The form was in academic terms a second set in a comprehensive. I had already noticed her ability to concentrate when many around her were distracted: when I set the class a poem to write on a storm (giving the alternative of descriptive prose) she seemed to be silently fighting with her material as she sat there; and when I read the result, created in about half an hour in front of me, I was shaken.

STORM

It arrived in the west burdened with anger
but remained quiet at first
then it whispered
low and warnful
eyes turned upwards
and knowing glances were made
Its anger grew worse and it made it known
It needed space to console itself
the sun turned in and gave it its way
engulfing the sky it turned it black
and continued its raging
then suddenly
it let loose
and emptied every hidden feeling
on the streets.

A nice piece but little there to interest Shakespeare, I hear you say. The next two entries will carry the two other poems I received from her. An Afro-Caribbean girl (of Jamaican heritage I believe) Orchyd had a dramatic gift, such as to make a journey of experience complete and knowable, that is uncommonly rare. I may say I have always loved this poem's first line.

People, people everywhere
March 15ᵗʰ 2021

(continued) At some point I asked Orchyd if she would, in her own time, write a poem with no time constraint. I wanted her to be free to let an idea develop, and said it could be any length she liked. I told her it didn't matter if she didn't write one; and not to be worried about asking if she wanted help, or just discussion, during the writing. She did not ask for either, and five days later turned up with an untitled piece that surprised me by its length. She was shy, and rather pleased at my surprise. She said it had taken her two evenings, working about two hours in each; and that she was not happy with all of it, but liked parts. At which point I took it away and read it.

People, people everywhere
A thousand beings
their faces portray nothing. Expressionless!
blanketed in their personal affairs
they drift into their chosen way of life
  Eyes that see
  but become blind
  hearts that feel but soon turn to stone
  Minds that store
  but eventually throw out

their stock when viewed under light
But my mind screams for help
I carry the past
And make supports for the future
For me there is no present
Every forthcoming second is the future
which turns into a wasted or
cherished memory
decisions to make every minute
every hour
I spend my most treasured hours bent over my shaft
  in the big machine called life
    And my heart cries out for freedom
But if I had complete freedom
    could I endure it
The self centred blank faced forms
are a great part of life
    my life
They cause me to hate
They cause me to love
They create situations which make me
think and consider.

There is the poetry of adults, and of adults half-formed; this is the latter and to me it is touched with greatness. When I first read it I put it aside for a day or two and tried to eradicate my first impression, but the statement is inescapable. Since it was written there has been a vast mass of published poetic output, of the senior variety, which may say any amount in any number of ways, but tends to undergo a lesser journey. Over the years a remarkable amount of outstanding poetry of the young has come my way, and especially at the outset of my career. But no other piece I think, written by young or old of the last half-century, has startled me as this did and does still. In its own way it crosses a waste land.

The lights of day appeared
March 16th 2021

(continued) The third and last poem I received from Orchyd was at the very end of term and of my time at that school. There were no more lessons with her class and she passed it to me in the corridor, and we didn't have a chance to talk about it. Later she wrote me a letter to do with it: a neighbour had died, leaving his wife and family. Orchyd and her mother knew the family well, and would borrow and lend tea, sugar etc. Orchyd said she wrote the poem all out at once, and later in the letter said that what she thought was special about poetry was its freedom. The principle was also apparent in her spelling, but it was worth the trouble to decipher it (though 'recite' gave me a hard time). Again there was no title.

    The lights of day appeared
And there is a debt to pay, the debt of being alive
        Afternoon at last
Even the sun looks weary
And almost unnoticed it sinks
                deeper deeper
    Another portion of the debt is paid
    And the debtor looks homeward

Behind bricks they comfort each other
    with word and action
Behind bricks they torment each other
But no matter how great a debt one day
    It will be paid
When one has paid his last debt
  And his feet turn homewards for the last time
  And his last words are spoken
They all stand and stare
    stare if they must
  but why with sadder eyes
  why the carefully chosen words
This debtor has now received his receipt
  He is now content and at ease
    He can now live live live.

This time, on first reading, I was anything but startled. The piece simply takes one along with it. But I was again amazed, at how much she was able to say, as at her means of saying. The beauty of the metaphor, the quiet clarity of the music, what a gift is there.

I did not stay in touch with Orchyd. I answered her letter and we left it at that. She was surely right to note the freedom of poetry as its special quality. But who has the skills to harness it? It is why I think the bard of bards might have nodded approvingly, if he could have seen those few untidy sheets of paper.

Just a Stone
March 21st, 2021

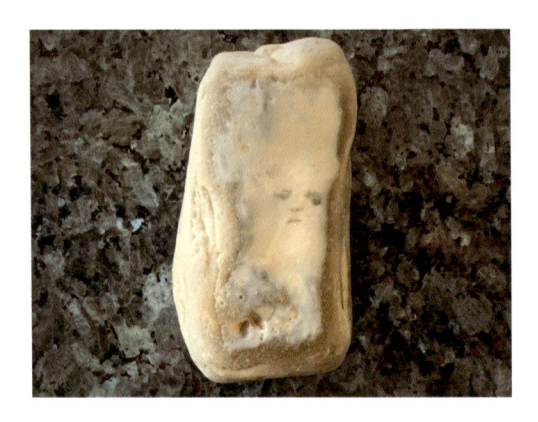

J ust a stone glistening in the wet. As I walk along the shore in a light afternoon mist any number of unusual glints in the shingle catch my eye and now and then I investigate. This to my surprise has a face.

It could be an Old Testament prophet's. It could be a face from a far older time, a shock of hair above and beard below. I take it home, leave it on my desk and am taken aback the next morning to find the face gone, that suggestion of a rugged countenance dried and faded out. What was at least in my imagination a driven force is now a blank, vaguely oblong-vertical patch of white.

Under the tap it comes back, the two half-shut eyes, the left with an alternative by it of a glaring wide-open one, the dots of nose and mouth. We're conditioned to see the human face, the human form. As a young boy I woke up in the small hours to see a giant's arm in the room. I watched it till the light revealed one of the beds in the dormitory. As a student later descending one of the great hills of Galloway with a friend I turned and saw a mist crawling over the top towards us. As we scooted down I had the image in my mind, and have it to this day, of a giant's thumb.

I pick up my stone and wonder what mountain it came from, what an inconceivable voyage it has been on, what a magical chemistry binds it together. And just as it takes me far back, so also far forward. What other entities will host these atoms? Will it splinter, smash, dissolve? Will it wedge back within some deep surround? Will it keep its form and face as it is, maybe till after the human face is gone?

I think of the tidal ripple washing over it countlessly. The rays of an afternoon mist that touched it for another magical construct to paint a face on, merely out of his imagination. He too suddenly knows of the tremendous odyssey of matter, wave after wave passing over him, through him, beyond him as he too is erased. For an instant the man he saw far back on a tiny sliver is real, then gone.

I know this man. I am this man.

Day of Reflection
March 23ʳᵈ 2021

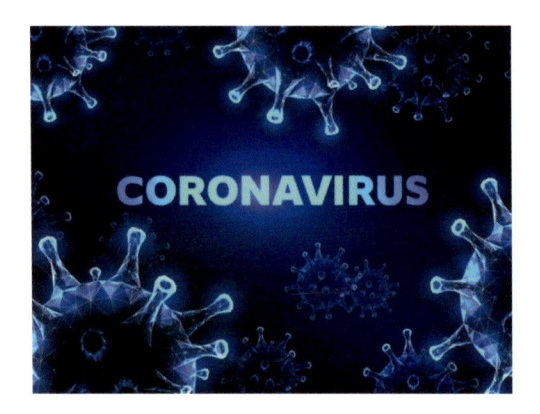

I can't speak for others. The altered experience of so many, across a harshly punctuated year, has been altogether different from mine. An older person, on his own but with family living near, I've had it easy: too easy in a way. Furlough money for doing nothing – how I need to get back to my one day a week teaching! – no immediate caring duties, the odd minor health issue attended to by the NHS in spite of their screaming overload – so one has drifted along. But within a bubble of comparative security my teeth have been gritted, like everyone else's. On this anniversary of the first lockdown, and waiting for the lifting of the third, the idea of a day of reflection has been promoted – not that many will have time for more than a few minutes of it. I think I've been most conscious of the mental frenzy this virus will have established in a million individual lives left without support.

It will rage for some time. Outwardly people will welcome the return to "normality" that it is hoped will soon take firmer root than before; within there may well be a legacy, a scar. After the War the business of practical reconstruction took first place. The unconscionable trauma of hardship and loss was addressed to an extent by an instinctive drive to build a new country with vital social reforms. That won't happen this time except in a kind of wishful thinking: it will be business as usual and in their own way people will – or will not – come to terms with all that has happened.

But I can't speak for them. For me, I shall have to somehow falteringly climb out of a valley I really don't want to look back on, an abyss of all that has not happened. Nature abhors a vacuum: I have become too comfortable doing nothing, perfecting a strategy of idleness. Perhaps I shall throw myself into a radical writing venture, entailing a deal of travel (even if without departing these shores, for the time being). Such a project has in fact long been on my mind. Perhaps I shall slide ever more gently into the rut of age. I hope it will be something nearer the former, for like everyone else – and here I know I can speak for all – I just want to put this damn time behind me.

The Flower Stand
March 25th 2021

How to describe a breath of pure pleasure, such that a sudden woodland grove that drew me into its wild orbit is for a moment not even seen? Just a breath, a scent for the ages, as I wheel round behind the church on my way down a small road to the sea. The sea air has the salt of wind and life and time, it's irreplaceable, always faintly epic; but this whiff of a secret garden has something richer, wilder, exquisitely subtle. A single breath once savoured I let my eyes – which have not closed, merely shut their sense away – take in the source. A controlled explosion, a composed riot of colour. An Aladdin's Cave.

The colours march up, at once present themselves; in their overlapping groupings and assortments of growth they cluster-bomb the mind with delight. But there are more modest shapes and stems, that wait to be noticed or not, it seems; a lilliputian forest of leaf-offerings, resting in among the loud blooms. Such delicate grace and sharpness, such toughness, such translucence, such a palette of green shades. They are the gentlemen, to my old-fashioned eye, in some wonderfully wind-strewn dance-hall of courtesy, among the ladies of light.

Reluctantly I turn from what has been for a space a rich beat of existence, and find myself out in the unadorned open, moving down the small road to the sea. It's good to look back on the moment, to have taken that breath of life . . . to have dawdled past a flower-stand.

Sooner or later
March 29th 2021

Sooner or later we have to stop condemning people for their thoughts.

Sooner or later we have to understand that the basis of religion is story not fact.

Sooner or later I'm going to have to clean the crumbs off the toaster tray.

Sooner or later Manchester United will find a manager to bring back their mojo.

Sooner or later a pig's ears will flap languorously through the air.

Sooner or later political cultures of West and East will learn to engage more profitably with the defence mechanisms of their adversaries.

Sooner or later the table-tennis club down the road will re-open and I can work on my backhand.

Sooner or later, if the world's going to bear up, we will have to think of 'alternative approaches' first and 'adversaries' second.

Sooner or later people who tend to opinionate should start to listen to themselves.

Sooner or later we have to ditch, or at least learn occasionally to discard, the rose-tinted spectacles by which we cannot help but romanticise our own position.

Sooner or later I'll meet a woman to wake to the dawn with and dance down the evening sky together.

Sooner or later at least I can get a haircut.

Sooner or later.

Dirge against the Dons
March 30th 2021

It climbs atop a precipice
where lesser minds have tumbled down;
it clings on to a benefice
in Oxford or in Cambridge town;
it's at a summit: all else is
pyramidically inclined:
and there it sits. I tell you this:
I loathe the academic mind.

It stands in gentle emphasis
of a post-post-doctoral gown,
and nods, and blows itself a kiss;
and quickly sits; for it must drown,
were that frail footing once to miss,
and slither and sink into a blind
uneducated dim abyss.
I loathe the academic mind.

It gleams in mental avarice,
and dreams of a philosopher's crown;
it sits bemused in ignorant bliss;
it is not emperor but clown;
for each don dons an artifice
to hide from life (as if confined
within a snug parenthesis).
I loathe the academic mind.

Reader, this aint "analysis" –
but a dig of a poetic kind
to give vent to a prejudice.
I loathe the academic mind.

Let bishops fianchetto…
April 5th 2021

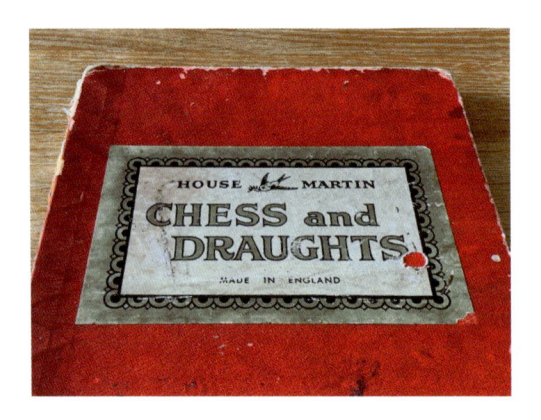

It's been with me a fair old time now, a knowing silent companion to my competitive niggle and lack of savvy in getting things done. Back in the day, when I was about 16, my sudden notoriety as chess secretary gave rise to a Votes for Chessmen campaign in a school mock General Election. Black-and-white-squared designs began to appear on posters, and asked for a slogan I came up with some doggerel instead:

Let bishops fianchetto,
send pawn on queenward trek,
applaud me *allegretto*
for I've discovered check!

The campaign soon petered out but my attachment to the game has never quite left me, though I play rarely enough these days. Yet even at school I lagged behind in one essential aspect: learning the theory. Openings and end-game in particular demand some work behind the scenes, but I have always preferred to play by instinct. Looking at the old miniature battle-field now I feel a pang of guilt. It's been with me all these days, it has hosted any number of glorious struggles … but perhaps it was due a little more expertise.

I took it with me to India where I lived in Kolkata for over a decade and unfolded it time and again on a table in the garden of the Fairlawn Hotel in Sudder Street, where I would go of an evening to drink gaseous beer. Between the honking of crows (one flapped down once onto the table next to me to snatch a crumb and upset someone's drink) and the raucous beeps of cars, I and a friend would play our hearts out as day turned to sudden night and the world fell away. Back in England I lost the board for a time – it had been picked up by someone at a school chess club I ran – and I made a passionate plea in an assembly for its return. What was it worth to anyone else? Whereas for me its marks of age were scars of battle, Victoria Crosses, win or lose. I was ridiculously delighted when it was anonymously returned.

As an author too I have lacked savvy. The background work needed to enable publication, or to consolidate what of that there has been, has not matched the need. But I have written my books, as I have played my games, following hunches, invisible patterns, watching combinations settle in front of me out of thin air. Words are my pieces of thought, and if I have not played the game to my and their best advantage in the public arena, at least where it most truly matters, I hope to have handled them more as they deserved. Seen or not, the finished poem on the sheet of paper, where the opposition has only been myself, has not lost the battle, nor when I go, the war. In some sense it will stand.

And what a time I've had, letting those delightful patterns compose themselves. Short struggles, long struggles, much rejected and lost, but every now and then a fluent passage of play finding its way. It is really a battle with Time itself then that is not lost.

And so my temporary self looks at a battered old acquaintance with a click of understanding. At once it seems to tell me off for overthinking my position. I see no more than a much-used, even treasured, somewhat ancient House Martin chess and draughts board.

Shiva

April 6th 2021

It's fifteen years since I returned from a long stay in India. While there I came to feel attached, in the very lightest of ways, to certain Hindu divinities. I did not "believe" in them but they were there: though merely characters in a story in one sense, they were real or half-real in another; and the link I felt with each at the time, hidden and elusive as it was, was indissoluble. With Shiva it still is.

Of Kali and Durga and Saraswati I shall talk another time. These three Goddesses variously enriched my stay and reinforced the flimsy structure I spent inner time in, so to speak; I owe them a lot. They are distant family now, though Kali especially is in my thoughts at times. But I have no need of a visible reminder of any, whereas the icon of Shiva on the shelf of an open cupboard is as part and parcel of the make-up of my flat as the photographs of my mother and father on the mantelpiece.

The stories of Hinduism are truer than most, perhaps than all the other major religious narratives, for behind the literal acceptance of ritual is a story-line fondness of the imagination. By which I mean a willingness to entertain the superhuman life-detail of deities as in some sense on a par with our own. It could have gone one way, it could have gone another. There is no grovelling diminution of the human but rather a touch of empathetic co-experience. As perhaps with religions of old and of less "advanced" communities now, a free-play aspect makes for a passing sense of identification that is truer to life than something more imposed.

As it may be. In Shiva's case it is his energy that, coupled with what it is directed to, can seem to confirm and direct my own micro-dot charge. In his shadow on the shelf he's as intent and sure-footed as ever, orchestrating some of the notes even of my existence in the furious ease and balance of his dance. I let him get on with it but it's good to know he's there.

Shiva
April 7th 2021

(continued) Shiva is one of the great triumvirate of Hindu deities. Brahma is the Creator, Vishnu the Preserver and Shiva the Destroyer. He destroys to make way for new creation; he is the god of dance, of time too. The male force in pure form his body is at times a pillar of fire, extinguished only by the vessel of Durga, his wife and the mother-goddess. Kali is his wife too; she is Woman in her absolute power. So is Parvati his wife, who manifests a lovely and delightful femininity. Yet (to me at least) all the wives are one. Hinduism is remarkable for a kind of divine chemistry here and there in the pantheon, so that one personality can be almost an allotrope of another. Yet each is separately free in itself, known and loved as itself, and sometimes feared.

I would not say I fear Shiva but I would not wish to speak too familiarly of him. I have unfinished business with him; everybody does. He is at once the householder and the detached yogi, absorbed in meditation. But he is also possessed of an entirely superhuman power. His throat is blue with swallowing poison that would have destroyed every last thing on Earth. Yet it is as lord of the dance, of time too, that his figure seems to carry the glimpse of a speaking significance at times, as I pass it on its shelf in the shadows.

There are scholars to pronounce on every imaginable aspect of divinity but I say, take these things as one will. As dance supremo Shiva has all the energy in the world. He may if one so wishes speak of the balance in the universe, he may dance to the music of the spheres; but for me it is the energy in all things, their making and unmaking and all their doing, that he reflects. While as lord of time I suspect him of knowing things we cannot know yet if ever. There is a vexed question of relationship in the material world that modern physics is just beginning to lay a hand on; with his extra pair of arms Shiva has it effortlessly in his grasp. Behind it all the small figurine on the shelf somehow sends me a signal of security, in the sense of being free from care; though why I do not know.

Mrs Tinckham and Mrs Canuticacq

April 9th 2021

One has a record and music shop not so far from where I live. Or at least her name is given to it: when I asked inside once for information as to the glorious shop title I met a blank; it was taken on with the premises, it seemed. For a long time as I used to pass it there was something in my mind, another name, another shop? . . . at last there it was.

Mrs Tinckham has a shop in Iris Murdoch's first novel, 'Under the Net'. I was entranced by the book and have always regarded it as her best, marvellous as her later novels are in patches. It's a dusty corner shop in central London that stocks newspapers and a variety of this and that, yet never seems to sell anything. The good lady spends her time looking after cats and customers, the latter coming to talk, to confide in her, to store drink for out-of-hours refreshment, to lodge articles of personal value . . . really to be looked after. She is the soul of discretion, seeming to be merely motherly in a rather vacant sense, but sleepily lightning-sharp and understanding everything, even in a way life itself. I have always loved the c in her name – perhaps ridiculously I feel the book would be a different one without it. The occasional repetition of 'Mrs Tinckham' in certain passages makes for a gently insistent lulling effect that is wakeful at the same time, to add a poetry of its own.

The record shop surname breathes mystery and mastery, to my ignorant ear and eye: no doubt to its owner and her compatriots it's as natural as daylight. But for a small shop to hang out such a shingle, as it were, tells of a buccaneering spirit: in the imagination the name goes sailing into the commercial capitals, a metaphor for the trading outreach and burgeoning wealth of mankind. Whatever the fortunes of the original establishment may have been in drab reality, 'Mrs Canuticacq's Emporium' is second to none. It is a three-word poem.

One of these magical stores exists in fact and the other in fiction. Of one the magic is in the name, while the owner of the other in her understated way is as real to me as any fictional character. While only the one emporium is out on the road, somewhere the two are side by side in a byway of the mind; where either operation is run by a presiding genius of a right royal distinction, in nature as in name.

Prince Philip
April 10th 2021

I don't know if he knew Norman Tebbitt. I imagine they may have met a few times. What I do know is that each man sacrificed an outstanding career prospect to support a woman, did so with unfailing dedication, and saw the job through.

Lord Tebbitt of course had a fine run as a politician up to the Brighton bombing of 1984 (that left his wife paralysed), and still holds a prominent position in public life. Other things being equal he may well have stood for the Conservative leadership after Mrs Thatcher left the scene, and may very well not have won it: the man who is supposed to have barked "On yer bike" to someone looking for work in his home area, though the story is apocryphal, had a deserved reputation for brusqueness. But almost certainly he would have had a longer Cabinet run than he did, and (in his own eyes at least, which is the point here) might have contributed more to the public life of his country. Simply, he made time to care more for his wife. More carers could have been found but the personal factor was all-important. She died late last year after 36 years of paralysis and 64 of a close marriage.

Prince Philip was also peremptory at times, and seems to have had a comedian's timing for a string of caustic-lite remarks, of which my favourite is his response once to a journalist's query as to the anxiety younger members of his family must be causing him. "Well, what were we supposed to do? Strangle them at birth?" But there was nothing offhand about his role as consort. The stellar naval career he might have enjoyed vanished, and as the background half of a quite splendid partnership, he has surely set the defining mark for a husband's support.

Lord Tebbitt's story moves me. Prince Philip's stuns me. Yet how often have women given their all for a husband's needs? Men of the world, take note.

Peace
April 12th 2021

I hate Silence most of all,
wherever it is I yell, scream and call . . .

So wrote Chief Rabbi Kimbal (Hallelujah) O'Neil, as he styled himself on another piece of work I was rather taken by. Entitled 'Snow' it began,

Round about January it falls
At Big Ben, Parliament and St Paul's . . .

Kimbal was a 14-year-old hell-raiser who loved words. But not for their own sake alone: he could think. Here is the end of a prose piece on 'Colour'.

'Colour is of the misformed, that which has colour is not perfect for each colour is more perfect more ugly than the other, the perfect has no colour, for colour is imperfect by itself, colour first must be made beautiful then combine with all other colour to form the perfect, the perfect as we do not yet know, the perfect which is yet to come, but for now we must put up with what we have, the white, the blue, the colour.'

When 'Peace' appeared as one of the alternatives on the blackboard I half expected him to lay into it as with 'Silence', in the unspoken classroom war that lay between us like a challenge. He did choose it and this is what he brought to my desk.

Peace is a walk by a stream
in summer with only the birds
Peace can't be touched
only to be enjoyed but never held
Peace is peace and only that
Peace cannot be seen or heard
for if it could peace would be no more
To know but not to know
For Peace is an essence
a secret beautiful essence
and the essence is
    Peace.

The natural impatience which possessed him continued to wreak havoc in many of my lessons; but Kimbal – who may well be retired by now – epitomises for me a type of pupil I came to know well, and (at least in retrospect) enjoyed teaching more than any other. The recalcitrant gifted, who made my life hell, and every now and then lit up the sky with their work. I wish him a richly hell-raising retirement.

War
April 13th 2021

At another school in those early days of teaching I was rocked back on my heels somewhat by a discursive, ranging poem that reminded me of the sweep and directed power of Orchyd's poems (see entries beginning page 40). Janet Morgan was also of Afro-Caribbean heritage: I mention it as I have occasionally wondered what I would find if I went out and taught in those islands. Teenage poetry, in its unexpectedness, can break a kind of sound barrier: suddenly as adults we find ourselves listening to a voice of innocence and experience at one, and uninhibited by fashion. Janet finds a path for herself rather than follow the style of another. She was I think fifteen years old.

War

Nature created the earth
to give mankind his birth
man created machine,
machine to cook
machine to subtract
machine to build
machine to destroy
men fight with guns and bombs

while their children and wives
afraid and hungry,
hope and pray
each and every day
for peace.
The peace they had when
the slosh and mud, was green grass
when the unhappy and bewildered
faces, wore smiles that would
crack a mountain
when the dusty lifeless sun
lashed down on the world, and
broke its beams into a trillion
crystal flakes,
when the tuneless voices
which sang hymns and prayers
were exciting and alive
and clear and bright.
The birds which once sang
at Christmas
are now part of the mud
dead bodies float aimlessly
on the river Nile
and cries of anguish and pain
and heartache
stretch through the hospitals
to the rooms, where the
blood-stained sheets
wait impatiently to be washed.
The sound of death
and noiseless suffering
glides through the living cemetery.

Shirley Williams
April 16th 2021

Since Harold Wilson stepped down there have been few leaders of the Labour Party worthy of the name. Several outstanding personalities have been overlooked and partly as a result the Party has lost its way somewhat. There is one way, and one way only for it to change and grow with the time so as to reflect an undying truth: that civilisation has been, and always will be, built on labour of an unglamorous kind. It has to honour the unadorned reality of work and care and sacrifice, that costs life after life after life.

Roy Jenkins had oratory and flair, Denis Healey a capacious intellect and force, Margaret Beckett a quiet yet commanding presence, David Owen a charismatic energy. Alan Johnson authentically reminded one of the central Labour message, with not a hint of shrill ostentation; Harriet Harman was and is brisk and to the point; Hilary Benn has matured into someone on the verge of true leadership; Emily Thornberry could become a blistering fighter for the cause. While David Miliband had that elusive quality of being at the centre of the argument, until perhaps understandably he turned his back on Westminster.

Why has not a single one of these people been entrusted with the Party? Beckett and Harman have been stand-in leaders for a few months only. Several might have made a perfectly adequate Prime Minister. But the greatest loss to the country's political life in my lifetime, as I see it, has been the under-use of Shirley Williams, who died the other day.

Such a composed, lucid intellect; such warmth combined with a crisp accuracy that could not have failed to make headway. I have the image in my mind of a plough cutting through soil. This is the Labour Party, in slow motion, as it should be: but it has stalled. Before she left it for the SDP and then the Liberal Democrats, Shirley Williams did much to stake her claim but little for herself. Had she led the Party, and indeed the country, she may or may not have made a success of it. Quite possibly she may not have been able to allow for the element of the irrational in politics, that Wilson was somehow at home with, as too is the present Prime Minister it seems; an invaluable gift for those in power. But Mrs Thatcher did well enough without it, and Shirley Williams might have found her own way of keeping a steady line. She seemed to carry a vision with her, and cut through to the nub of things. At the same time she was non-dismissive and ready to listen. In my view she was as fine a leader as this country has not had.

Surviving the Death Railway
April 20t^{yh} 2021

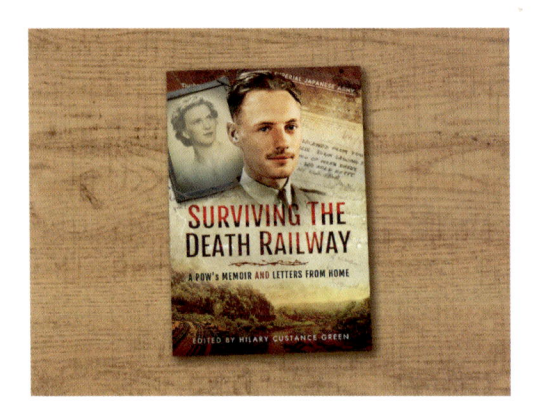

In July 1941 Captain Barry Custance Baker, 26 years old, set sail for Singapore. In charge of 27 Line Section, a communications unit of 72 men, he left behind in England his wife Phyllis and their infant son Robin, to set up telephone routes to airstrips in the Malayan jungle. The Japanese overran Malaya, he was taken prisoner, and from November '42 he was made to work on the infamous Burmese-Thailand railway. He survived, though barely at some points, and returned to wife and son after the War. After his death (at 94) his daughter Hilary found an assortment of cards, telegrams and letters, mostly between her parents but also between her mother and relatives of the other men in 27 Section: she had gone to extraordinary lengths to obtain what information she could about all the missing men. Hilary put together a record of a shattering war story, a delicately charged and beautiful story of love, together with the imprint of a web of darkness, as so many people at home carried on in a kind of half-life, waiting for news.

As well as by letters that did and did not arrive (some emerged after liberation) the book is informed by excerpts from an account of his war experiences Barry wrote in his eighties; as also by photos of many of the young men in the Section (several died out there). I read it slowly. It is a story of sheer damned endurance, both physical and mental, both in the prison camps and at home. But also of the delights of ordinariness

– Robin as toddler comes across in his mother's letters with a notable ebullience – while Barry has a great time acting in the (very) occasional dramatic productions the prisoners were able to put on. But swirling through and under everything is the current of a brutal horror, that can almost seem to be instinct in human affairs, and was relayed on by the Japanese military mindset of the time.

Such is the skill of the editor that one has a picture of her father's adult life from a 21-year-old meeting his future bride to shortly before he died, when for an hour or two he was trapped in a terrifying warp in time, and back in his head with his captors. But above all it is a story of activity, energy and love. It was not at the moments of dreadfulness but of its opposite, for which there is no name, that at times I shook with tears.

Warhol Immersive
April 22nd 2021

For a few weeks the newspaper picture's shuffled itself about on my desk, on top of this book, under that envelope. Kids having fun in a state-of-the-art 'immersive classroom . . . where the blank walls can be changed to provide a 360° educational experience'. What's not to like? Maybe nothing. But I find the picture disturbing.

It's not so much that I personally have no time for the lurid territory in the brave new world of art that Andy Warhol managed to stake out sixty years ago. So far as I can see he discovered nothing except a memorable way of making the utterly unoriginal appear original: a neat trick, and one carried on today by Damien Hirst among others. After all, the next fleeting mural image to materialise might be something genuinely intimate and provocative – perhaps Paul Klee's 'Ships in the Dark'. Rather I think it's as a reminder of a continuing situation that the scene slightly rattles me. Young children let into a secret, in the accompanying thrill of a modern magic classroom, that art can be as easy as anything – all you need is a new way to present something familiar. It plays to an element of instant gratification, in the culture they are growing up in, that is nothing new in itself, but way stronger than it used to be. And apart from tending to see what's going on (however briefly) as an anti-educational experience, I react

– I admit it – on a directly personal level. It's the con-artist getting away with it again.

Yet it's a delightful scene. Campbell's Soup Cans clatter silently against the walls of the mind, Marilyn flings a careless prettiness onto the air, the children are having a magical time. Who am I to judge? And who am I, as someone who remembers more ordinary classrooms from a time before Warhol hit the headlines, to feel a certain unease at the playthings of a richer age? But I do.

Jimmy White and world peace
April 23rd 2021

Back in the mid-seventies I was teaching in Balham, South London, and used occasionally to go after work to Zan's snooker hall in Tooting. On one visit I overheard a group discussing the exploits of a certain Jimmy White, a 13-year-old who used to bunk off from a school nearby to take on all comers, knocking in centuries with a cheerful ease, and already something of a legend.

I followed his career with a certain interest. I used to watch the game on TV at home with my two sons, to my wife's wearied amusement. Once we went in the sitting-room to find the TV on and proceeded to watch a deserted snooker-table for several seconds, till we realised the screen wasn't on … but a cut-out of green baize-like material was on it, cunningly attached. Point made. Another time the three aficionados were outraged at the interruption of the World Championship Final by an altogether less newsworthy item, the siege of the Iranian Embassy in London. Who wanted to see gunmen crawling along window-ledges when Alex Higgins and Cliff Thorburn were locked in a shoot-out of their own?

By now the young maestro was well on his way. White recorded his first World Championship final in 1984 and reached the same point five times more – in five successive years! – without once finding the win.

He has won other events galore and has always been a favourite with the public. A massé shot he played in competition in 1993 has been watched in awe millions of times. An easy-going TV pundit these days, he is loved for his straightforwardness, his knowledge of the game, his past brilliance ... and somehow for that run of failures at the last fence, too. He still enters the World Championship Qualifying event each year, and what wouldn't we all give to see him make the last stages again ... perhaps ... who knows ... could it be?

No, it couldn't. But as the fans return to the (wonderfully-named) Crucible in Sheffield for the current World finals, imagine the moment if the truant lad could at last lift that silver cup! What would that say to the gods and demons who blithely cannon and ricochet through the lives of us all? Wouldn't it be the one event to bring world peace to the table?

Words
April 24th 2021

Words are like elastic bands. With the difference that they don't break if stretched too far.

Consequently their usefulness can be overrated. They can seem to hold something in place when they don't.

Take "life after death". The word 'life' is there, meaning the opposite of what it does otherwise, something that ceases at death. So it's there in a sloppy, floppy way, not doing justice to the concept but obscuring it.

Take (poor thing) Schrödinger's cat. Quantum interference means it's in a state of being both dead and alive (or alternatively both asleep and awake). Only it doesn't. A picture is lifted from (what we know of) the sub-atomic world and imposed on the super-atomic, where it does not fit. But the words used seem to suggest the fit is there. The thing is, progress is being made in this case.

It's a belly-flop rather than a clean dive into a new area. To go further, we need to take more closely into account the main instrument we use to get along with.

Words are our most important invention by far. But even though the meaning of so many is changing all the time, under our noses, we tend to think of them as little fixed pieces of wire. We loop them over a concept or idea and imagine they hold it in place. Whereas they stretch to fit the way the idea stretches in one context, or flop round it if it shrinks in another, and accuracy goes to the dogs. Or it stays with the (poor old) cat but not with those who talk about it. Schrödinger put forward his paradox in 1935. Maybe it's time we brushed up a little on its appearance.

Roads
April 26th 2021

There must have been a year of lockdown days by now in England and on most of them I've walked to the sea and back, in and out of the same net of roads. With the reduced variety in one's general experience of being out and about, some things come through a little more, and one for me has been this simple prop and support from the past, maintained in the present, and occasionally tweaked for the future. The ever-present stamp of a community under one's feet, the local roads.

At any one time, however chance or loose-knit the community may be, its groundwork gives it the scope to flourish, in a sense keeps it going. In the country the continuity with the past tends to be more settled; yet in any old town what a scent – or whiff – of the past there can be in a street or a street's name. History is with us.

One can take it back and back. These tracks thumped out by feet, boots, machines are in our evolutionary DNA. Ancient ways abound. Once I walked the length of what may be the oldest road in England, the Ridgway, with one of my sons. Now a smart-road technology is thrusting our bipedal race ever more swiftly into the future, it seems; but as self-driven cars sweep us ahead on a freewheeling way from A to

B, somehow a connection is still there with the wayfarers of old. After all they took on the same journey.

Birds have their sky-roads, arboreal animals their tree-roads, insects their trails. The touch of an Earth-map is in us as in them, a tangible and patterned link to our geographical existence as scampering beings.

So in lockdown my thoughts have been freed up a little, treading a new path along with the old.

Clouds
April 27th 2021

If I were to go blind I think I'd like to pause on them, and reflect. They might be a means, in the mind, of saying something about visual beauty, which can be too much *there* to ponder successfully, in the line of direct and available sight.

Of course by "successfully" I mean "to my satisfaction". Aestheticians will have resolved the enigma thousands of times in the past and will go on doing so thousands of times in the future. However, I have an idea how I might begin.

How is it that the spectrum of sunlight, broken to sky-blue and to cloud-white, can offer a notion of harmony? And of course it's nothing, really, to do with peace. A raging storm can be – is – beautiful. Vyasa, the author of the Indian epic 'Mahabharata', finds beauty in the blood and gore of a battlefield, with the eye of a detached artist summoning us to the scene.

It's something to do with contrast. It's the white against the blue – or indeed dark clouds against the lightning – that can pluck at the mainstream of awareness, spur on a ripple of attention, lead up to an encounter. A sense of a textural difference, too – and what textures! – draws on a faculty for wonder, that no doubt it has helped to develop.

Together with the sunset and the sunrise, the sight and passage of clouds must have done something to humanise the species early on.

It's something to do with motion. Clouds are here and gone. As not only are we but significantly, our thoughts. From birth till death the mind is never still.

It's something to do with the spirit that recognises and engages with the circumstance of life. What we find beautiful has allowed us a deeper engagement.

In blindness – after sight – one might or might not be closer to a mystery by reflection, by not being too much *there*. Perhaps the idea of the transient beneath or within the everlasting has something to do with it. I daresay I've got it all wrong as usual. With respect, then, to the blind, I'll take my head out of the clouds. Right now it's too vivid and fresh a day to be thinking.

Winds
April 29th 2021

'Who has seen the wind? Neither I nor you,' says Christina Rossetti, and she has a point. Even in a twister you only see water droplets. Once I got caught in a dust-storm in Kolkata, and another time in a snowstorm north of Glasgow, but I can't say I saw more than millions of manic particles each time, though I felt the force behind them plenty. Understandably poets tend not to tackle the wind head-on. How does one engage with that vanishing-act, that power?

Ted Hughes has quite a crack at it. 'This house has been far out at sea all night, The woods crashing through darkness, the booming hills,' he starts an almost frightening filmic description in verse. Yet I prefer Rossetti's child-like poem introduced above. The trouble with all Hughes' verse is that you can't take the man out of his work and experience it as everyman (please take the term as inclusive): there's a machismo label over the lot. Whereas the Bard has King Lear shouting 'Blow, winds, and crack your cheeks! rage! blow!' and the words operate entirely free of their author, and this is so whether he is presenting a character on stage or his own (apparently) in the Sonnets. My two favourite poetic wind-moments however are in a way more direct even than this.

'Ye motions of delight, that haunt the sides Of the green hills, ye breezes and soft airs,' wrote Wordsworth, and my mind somehow has a spot reserved for a wild and breathing great slope of grass. While I forever take my hat off to a single word of Dylan Thomas's. 'Especially when the October wind With frosty fingers punishes my hair,' he begins one of his poems, and whether or not he saw a lock of hair rising slightly and falling, in the shift and syllable-play of the first word, I see and imagine it.

I wondered about an image for this entry, and then remembered a time when I could see the winds. As a child I used to play mah-jongg and waited impatiently for the special tiles to come up of the flowers, seasons, winds and dragons. Maybe the magic in that game, building and dismantling a wall of ivory tiles, in touch with strange characters that meant more than I could know, prepared me just a little for a life of poetry. I'd like to think so.

E.B.B.
May 3ʳᵈ 2021

Christina Rossetti *(see last entry)* puts me in mind of Elizabeth Barrett Browning, whose poetry at its best I prefer to that of her husband Robert Browning. To my mind Rossetti and E.B.B. vie for the position of second best female poet in English, Emily Dickinson taking the honours with her breath-taking originality and verve. (Somehow one falls into the language of a Bake-Off competition, inapt beyond apology.) There are few immortal poems from any of these and only two I know of from E.B.B., of which most poetry readers know only one. 'How do I love thee? Let me count the ways' may be the finest sonnet written since the form's apogee in the 16th and 17th centuries. Everyone who thinks of her knows it. But 'Aurora Leigh', E.B.B.'s novel in verse, is little known and rarely mentioned now, and it's a masterpiece.

'There is not a dead line in it,' said the poet and critic Swinburne; and while a few passages may need re-reading to pick up the full story (at least I found so), I'd concur. The essence is an amazingly modern feminist statement, as incisive as Chaucer's Wife of Bath's Prologue is powerful. At the same time it carries a love story not untypical of its time. It was written mid-nineteenth century and does not shirk a certain sentimentality at the end, but my God it's a sentimentality that is earned.

It's long. Over eleven thousand lines of blank verse, in nine sections, it's not everyone's idea of a dip into a distant literary scene. And yet, with its beautifully-worked plot and scattered rich imagery, it's a swift enough page-turner.

But I have a problem I cannot solve, and it's summed up in the initials of the author's name. Why is it that in fifty years of teaching, the poetry in its true strength that I've come across in the classroom has almost always been from girls – and yet so few of the world's great writers have been women? Why does that confidence fall away? What is this appalling male near-hegemony of the *right* to create with the mind? Elizabeth Barrett Browning's reputation is far from what it was (when Wordsworth died she was considered for poet laureate) but her name may yet come to belie her initials. But will the blind force that can turn to genius continue to retreat from girls as they become women? Is it always more likely to settle in men? What is the element that holds it in place? Is it callousness?

Saraswati
May 4th 2021

She is the Hindu Goddess of knowledge and learning, of music and the arts, of the graces of the mind. Pronounced (by Bengalis) something like Shoro-shoti (short o's, soft t) her name means 'She of the drift of waters' and concurrently 'She who has speech'. The two together can almost mean poetry, as I choose to take it. At any rate there are times when I can feel under her wing.

She arrives (at wherever she is, say in a temporary temple or pandal put up during a festival) on a swan, which nestles by her, and she plays the veena, the ancient stringed instrument of India. That is where I became aware of her presence in the background, and never more tellingly than once when I was visiting a primary school in a village. A small field lay next to the school and at its centre was a small hut. When I asked its purpose I was told it was where children went alone to pray to Saraswati before their first reading lesson. The field and hut had no other use.

Education is valued in India as the privilege it is. On the goddess's special day (in January or early February) there may well be a small pile of books by her image (which will be everywhere). Perhaps it will include a dictionary. There will be a lotus and a priest will say prayers, and members of the public at a pandal or of a private household at an indoor shrine will join in. Saraswati is also the name of a river of ancient

India (long since dried up), and I sense a river's rippling movement somewhere at the heart of the educational ideal, however much at variance that may appear with the practice. In all schools in all countries a certain rigidity can as it were over-announce itself. But the goddess is not there for no reason.

In 'A Room of One's Own' Virginia Woolf speaks of "Shakespeare's sister". With an identical talent to his could such a one have emerged as he did? Then and now it's all too much of a man's world. But who knows what may come about in the future, with a figure like Saraswati at the back of it all?

The Satanic Verses
May 8th 2021

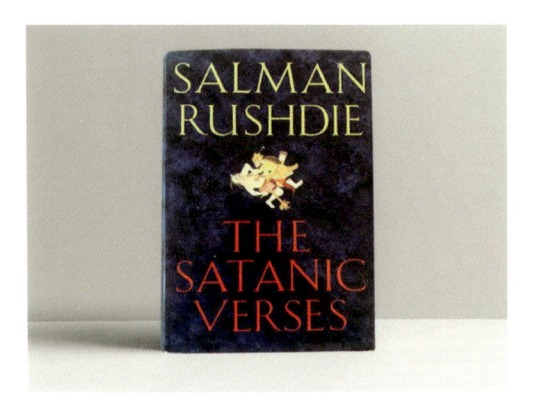

A savage episode tore across the face of Western culture a generation ago. Salman Rushdie published a novel and a few months later the Supreme Leader of Iran, the Ayatollah Khomeini, issued a *fatwa* calling for his death.

The book was felt to be deeply insulting to Islam and with reason. On the other hand a poem deeply insulting to many of the Christian faith, 'The Love that Dares to Speak its Name', was published in Gay News in the UK in 1976; and while an old law of blasphemy then still on the books allowed a prosecution to be brought, which succeeded in that a conviction was attained, no punishment was imposed and the outcry very soon died down.

I read 'The Satanic Verses' to see what the fuss was about. I found it a dreadful novel. It dabbles in magical realism, a literary genre I'm not a fan of; it comes over all normal and tender for a chapter near the end; and reverts, finally and forgettably, to a central strange-toned narrative, which to me was an incomprehensible howling in the wind. I echoed it somewhat as I used to groan while reading it. I didn't know I was doing this but my wife did – she'd yell from the other end of the house for me to put that damned book down. But I read every word.

Most who picked it up didn't. A journalist who'd reviewed it for a national newspaper told me he hadn't been able to make it to the end. (It was a positive review nonetheless.) And I met someone who'd been on a remarkable television programme about it. As the furore gathered pace the BBC had the idea of bringing a variety of people together in a Yorkshire farmhouse for a fortnight – young and old, Muslim and non-Muslim. They had all been given a copy and asked to read it before they started the brief communal experiment. She swore not a single one out of them all had managed to get through it.

I saw the programme and it was the most illuminating one of my life. At the beginning one of the numerous conversations shown gave us a young Muslim man, heavily bearded, shaking with rage at a smooth and sneering owner of a bookshop on the south coast. The youth wanted Rushdie killed and, it almost appeared, the bookshop owner, for insisting on a massive display of the book in his shop window. "It's my right, it'll get customers into my shop, there's nothing you can do about it." (Or words to that effect.) I was sickened by them both. At the end of the programme these two were shown again. The bookshop man said something like, "Well, I'll tell you what. I've eaten with you and other Muslims over the past two weeks, I've gone on walks with you, I'll tell you what I'm prepared to do. There's no way I'm not going to sell the book, but instead of a great stack of them in the window there'll just be one copy there – though it will be central. How about that?" His tone was condescending, still half-sneering, as if he was giving away the earth.

The violently-minded youth wept. He said, "Thankyou, thankyou, that's more than enough." I was moved. And for the first time I saw something clear. The defensive mindset that can bring the world crashing down upon itself and everyone else can be reached and, by extension, breached. An accommodation can be found. But there has to be a reaching out. However slight the gesture has to be *felt*. This is what the mindset craves, to *feel*. Then even a little – almost a nothing – can go a long way.

The Satanic Verses
May 10th 2021

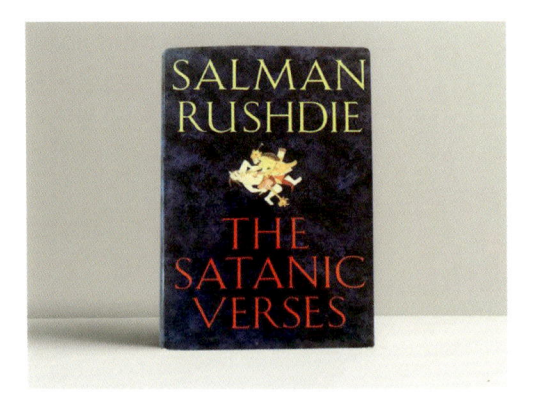

(continued) Rushdie was in hiding for years after the *fatwa* was issued and received sustained protection from the British police (whom he had caricatured in his novel as brutes, ironically enough). Technically he is still in danger. Meanwhile so-called identity politics is whipping up the idea of victimhood into a perfect storm of 'the little tremors of the mind and heart', to take a phrase of Auden's. There is suffering and there is suffering: a sense of proportion is being lost. I think of the bearded youth and the bookseller. The gargantuan offence taken by so much of the Muslim world, at what were only words used cleverly in a rather childish way, is altogether inapposite on the surface – but it springs from something that is nothing to do with a few naughtily-used words. At a deeper level it is understandable.

The action proposed – death – is an over-reaction, to put it lightly. But as a lashing-out from a tumbled, jumbled history of tribes and races in a head-on collision with the West – a pattern of centuries – it makes a kind of emotional sense. And this is what is so often forgotten in the weighing-up of rights and wrongs in flashpoints and confrontations large and small, with nations as with individuals. It is an emotional situation.

A gesture is needed, a gesture that is felt. The West is often technically in the right and emotionally in the wrong. It is consumed by a kind of narcissism whereby the headway it is making on its own is good enough, and its interest in other cultures is minimal.

To learn songs, prayers, poems and sayings in other languages would profit the learner and reach the heart of those for whom such things are their daily sustenance. The language of dance or of music also can speak across a divide. There is so much – so much – to be informed by, to learn.

It is the West that has to come out of hiding. Small advances can meet with tremendous results. Wary as I am of a culture that looks for micro-aggressions in its internal behaviour, I think it is worth looking out for a casual macro-aggression long in operation against the Orient at large. It must have been thirty years ago that I saw a complacent bookseller make the smallest of overtures to a wounded spirit and even so, to touch a nerve. It has taken me this long to realise I am that bookseller in my Anglophone complacency, in my European sense of a higher civilisation, in my Western prison. I hope my grandchildren, and their grandchildren, will know what to do, when the outside world comes battering at the walls.

Election Special
May 11th 2021

Following last week's "Super Thursday" democratic reckoning, the air is currently supercharged with electoral fall-out. I'm as excited as the rest of them, while wryly recalling Malcolm Muggeridge's remark that politics like sex has become an ersatz religion. Without reference to minorities and majorities, or to who is now councillor or mayor or MP for what or where, I thought I'd reflect on the mark the rite of passage itself leaves on one. It's at one and the same time a check-in to the counter of chaos and an alignment with a necessary re-ordering. After all, society has to change.

It scarcely seems to matter whether one actually votes or not (as I didn't this time). To an extent one is almost bound to be caught up in the operation, with the ever-slicker analysis of the media, the on-the-spot interviews, the travelling commentary with magic TV white-boards and surreal studio-floor lay-outs. The smash and crash of public personalities as they rise or fall. The sense of history in the making. One can delight in triumphs or fume at disasters, or simply gape at the circus: but at some slight level our empathy is stretched. These public figures take us a tiny bit of the way with them on their personal journeys. While great figures from the past of the various parties and political movements hover in the wings, or as it may be turn in their graves. Chaos is made out of order and order out of chaos.

As the dust-storm settles, and a briefly towering wave of mixed emotions begins to fall away, one has been touched again by an age-old sign, the imprint of one's land. The election is over. Whether or not one has cast a vote for a particular party or person, there has been a light branding. One marks the moment as it marks one. It is part of a process that must be.

Is it even worth saying?
May 12th 2021

THE SPECTATOR

Art has been touched by a dead hand. Let me offer an example. In 'The Spectator' each week are one or two short poems and a verse competition. The latter turns out by far the better art, even though it's for laughs and ephemeral. The so-called poems are slow-paced, weary, somehow deliberately unadroit so far as the old apparatus of poetry is concerned. What harmonies of word-arrangement they employ they do so as if by accident, almost apologetically, as if not wanting to be deterred from the quest, which tends to be a mental observation with little feeling attached. 'The London Review of Books' carries similar frozen snapshots, as indeed does the whole publishing world in these barren days in the case of poetry: it has become the standard, the norm. This is the world of modern art. It skirts the idea of beauty; it comes from and arrives at a dead end.

The weekly competition in 'The Spectator' throws the matter into relief. It is warmly, not coldly intelligent. I'm often lost in admiration at the sheer deftness on display of words and the ideas they carry. If only some of the regular prize-winners had given heart and soul to the business of "true art" and furnished the time with a cascade of inner exploration and discovery. But that word – cascade – gives the lie to the present set-up, which is more like a region locked in permafrost. Why go there?

And yet one should emphasise that the magazine itself (and so with the LRB) is far more part of the real world than its poems. It is communicative, witty, wide-ranging, above all part of an ongoing concern – as the mind is, as life is. Art of old (in whatever form) did not bring its journey to a sudden stop. To slam on the brakes, jam against the senses – sometimes almost before it has started – was not the way.

There are reasons galore for the modernist (post-modernist etc.) approach in art. Part of it is a skewed development from an original pointedness in the new artistic outlook that utilised the element of shock (and quite often, as it happened, the shock of humour). Part of it is that it taxes the artist's mind less now to create, the reader's (listener's, onlooker's) less to appreciate. Part of it is no more than the remorseless fist of fashion. The blanket of a timid artistic achievement covers the public arena, like a wan face. Those who could make a difference won't go there, and with reason. The blanket is immovable, it seems, and the fight to make even the tiniest impression, to be part of the living current, is a losing battle.

Some go there nonetheless. They have no choice.

Is it even worth saying?

The Spectator
May 14th 2021

THE
SPECTATOR

(continued) It's a good title for a magazine, as 'The Observer' is for a newspaper. One is presented with some sort of a re-cap of current affairs and as it were invited to attend a free-ranging debate, which is conducted generally from a particular angle but gives one at least an idea of opposing views. There is space (if a small one) on the letters page for a reader's contribution; and lighter pieces, including puzzles and competitions, while the time away. A good magazine is entertaining, informative, even necessary in its commentary – but non-urgent. A work of art, however light on the surface, is not non-urgent. It is vital, fresh, and stays so.

It is part of the living stream. The news media are a reflection of the stream in its larger scale. An individual life is more than that, in its small way it is no reflection but a part of the flow; and a work of art, imbued with its creator's vitality, immortalises that part. That is how the artist lives on. That may happen if in its perception, what it "says", the artwork is unique, as an individual is; and so as a unit of special awareness it too has an individual status. As such it is not cut off from its surround, existing merely in its own time-line and local appearance, but conveys a link at a deeper than everyday level to the current of life.

When a story ends there is the sense not of a sudden stop but a joining with ... a deeper narrative? One may simply call it a current. This is so for a child or an adult, and with a story or a poem, a piece of music or a painting or a sculpture, if there has been a certain kind of journey in getting to know it. To return to poetry, the "I" of the reader or listener of old is taken on a journey and liberated; but the modern concept of a journey in art is apt to lead up to or into a state of arrest. Then where is the current?

The fact is, the underlying assumption of modern art is that there is none. There is merely a passing series of phenomena. And the reader (listener, onlooker) tends to be no more than a spectator, as each observation is landed within a focal area, so to speak, and let lie. It is a cold, detached sort of business.

One becomes a viewer of unrelated perceptions. They may appear each to be unique but are so not as part of the uniqueness of life itself, but only in an unjoined-up way. With apologies to the admirable magazine, this is what its poetry – as virtually every poem that is published now – comes down to. The reduction of the individual to a camera or a recorder. The thinning-out of the blood to a watery nod. A mental pandemic has reduced the population of the world of art to the lonely satisfaction of a closed position. This is Art now and this is its Spectator.

The living stream
May 15th 2021

First I must remorselessly strip any religious connotations from the phrase. The stream is the current of life, with its chop and change and tidal flow, within which animate and inanimate are scarcely separate. Walking Hove shore, as I do most days, I find myself more and more at ease with the notion of movement at the back of everything, of 'the whole boiling', as Philip Larkin might have said. In a sense it is everything.

Which is why I feel the sense of "cut-off", so pronounced in modern art of all description, however much it may speak to a dislocatory effect in modern life, is fundamentally inapt. In the greatest works of modernism, Eliot's 'Waste Land' for instance, an extraordinary sense of continuity is discovered beneath the disjointedness. It is there in a final reaching-out (and it underpins the metre throughout, which is not as wayward as it seems). In the greatest stage tragedies, 'Oedipus Tyrannus', 'King Lear', it is there in the sense of a deepening play of the plot beyond, forever in lives at large. (Again, the idea of a continuous connective movement is carried in the form, in the immaculate use of hexameter or pentameter.) But such a bond with the invisible, so to speak, such a link to that which is always around us, is not limited to "great literature". A fifteen-year-old can find it as naturally as can anyone in modern times who is not persuaded by fashion or convention that it is wrong to do so.

Janet Morgan (see page 68) takes on a momentous event and the astonishment expressed at the end does not end there; it is a part of the world. While I did not want the title of this entry to be necessarily associated with religion, as it is often so used, here there is almost a live streaming of the principle I am trying to talk about. A work of art accumulates an imaginative truth that will interact, finally, in some way with the further surround.

THE BIRTH OF JESUS

The sly moon crept over the night
bringing with it, a gentle breeze.
Patient impatientness, and tender
suffering, held in its grip, the
blessing or the curse of the unsuspected.

Minds assemble and meditate
minds of noble men,
minds of peasants,
and even the minds of the fortunate
dead, that lie in peace and tranquillity beneath
poverty and cringing uneasiness.

But Ecstasy is born,
The city reincarnates itself,
Shouts and laughter ring out
from the lungs of the city,
shattering the stiff walls of silence.
The city has been blessed.

Ballad to the Pubs' Re-opening
May 17th 2021

Is that the open door of a pub?
  Is a night-reveller in there?
Can I go in and get some grub,
  and drink and eat without a care?
I think I'll have a syllabub,
  and a glass of insobriety,
and in the breath of a fresh hubbub
  I'll drink to the world's variety!

The land has been a desert scrub
  in the clutch of a wintry air,
a withered shrub, a dried tree-stub . . .
  which now is transformed everywhere.
This vision of Beelzebub –
  this dry rot in society –
is taken out by a nuclear sub.
  I'll drink to the world's variety!

All's fresh and new – and here's the nub:
  this shivering state we used to share –
the land of the two-metres snub –
  was in our souls. We did not dare
to clink a glass – ay, there's the rub
  to a too-prim propriety.
But the wheel's turning – we're at the hub –
  I'll drink to the world's variety!

Reader, I may be going to blub
  with joy and not anxiety.
Come join me in this old night-club!
  We'll drink to the world's variety!

Those dancing chips
May 20th 2021

Lift-off. In space. A familiar flight with familiar forces pinning one down. It could be an arcade game except that this is no flight simulator, there's something deadly in the air, it's life-and-death over a handful of gaudy discs. Maybe as much as several handfuls, a tray-load, more even, there's a fortune on hand, one has to kill, to triumph, to swindle, to outgun, to lull, to wait with intent, to strike – and to know when to fall back, to switch off, to let a skirmish go, to wait, to wait again, to strike and strike hard. These coins, these counters are the stuff of life, nothing in themselves but the only thing, the tumbling cascade at the back of it all, the gold-dust, the perfect solution. Manoeuvre. Wait. Take. Grab.

The instruments we fly with, the control panel, the apparatus at our finger-tips, thin slides of information with constantly changing values, numbers that perform acrobatics, colours and shapes that can mean nothing or the world, that can conjure up tricks out of this world, these are commonly known as the cards. They operate in pairs, threes, fives at the most, yet sometimes a single high card can win. Sometimes a paltry hand, with mixed colours and numbers that mean nothing, can knock out a state-of-the-art collection, if the first owner has touched the right invisible levers at the right time. It's a mind-game, this is the space we're in, ducking and dodging and diving and . . .

Delivering. And the little mountains grow. Or all is lost. Pack up. Go home. There'll be another time to take off, to creep up on the side, or simply to scythe in, carve through, swipe another's stack, round up the glittering piles. To win.

I'm back after a night of epic. Shooting-stars are in my mind, terrific wins and terrible losses, a fading picture of constellations, duelling swords in the air, distant explosions as other worlds have ignited to extinction, played their all and lost. Or they have usurped space-kingdoms, played a blinder, left contrails to linger of a glittering orbit, won the field.

My mind is no more than the green baize of a poker table. Nine hours at the feet of Lady Luck and I'm done. As I drift off all I see is that trim lawn, cards, cards falling like leaves, and at the back of it all a spinning wealth of air, those dancing chips.

George Street
May 25Th 2021

Tenderly it comes to life. A seagull perches on a shop-sign to survey the scene. The street has been silent too long, trapped in a hibernation from which it has struggled to awake at times, an unnatural near-death episode in its long history. Fourteen months of let-down, of lockdown, twice partially freed and twice re-frozen, sinking back into the chill of a slowed-up metabolism. And now something's happening. Everything's happening.

The same shop colours are quietly speaking, it seems; after the let-down, the lockdown, there's a subauditory clamour, a signalling, a quickening. I slowly walk up the pedestrianised precinct to let it come through. Barclay's cobalt blue, a jeweller's and pawnbroker's bottle-green, Santander's scarlet, Wetherspoon's dark navy blue. There's information in the air, I can feel it, for a moment I'm charged with it. After the lockdown, the lowdown. A barber's red-and-white stick of rock. A clothing store's olive green. An olive-tree outside it takes the signal, transforms it: suddenly it's there, the vociferous news, the leaves thrill to the wind, it's starting up again.

Some shops have failed. But the street has said something, not just for the current escape but for the driven current itself. Not just for the age but for the ages. I pass a busker with all the surrounding colours it seems, and then some. She's a one-woman street vaudeville, or voix de ville; the olive-trees have passed the signal on, for a second it's at full throttle, it's what I'm here for . . . I turn and make my way back.

Incredibly the seagull's still on the shop-sign. How long did all that take?

Manchester United
May 26th 2021

There they go. The dilettantes underperform again. Airily passing the ball around, waiting for a fairy godmother with size 10 boots to step in, fasten on a pass and actually crack a shot at goal. And so they lose the Europa League final to a team a good way south of them in talent and north in desire. It's the last match of the season and on paper they've done well, second in the Premier League after third last year. But they haven't done well. They haven't played to their strengths. They've coasted.

Only once this season have they not drifted about more or less incoherently for a time before being rescued by the undeniable skills of their forwards. That was against their "noisy neighbours", Manchester City, who were on a blinding winning streak at the time (and indeed ended up walking away with the top spot). United knew they had a match on and came out fighting. They clicked as a team, kept going, and won an outstanding game 2-0. Only then did they find their feet as the force they could be.

And the force they were, under the leadership of Alex Ferguson, he of the "noisy neighbours" aside. Since his reign they've been managed respectively by a staring-eyed Walter Mitty, an overgrown schoolboy, a plum pudding, a vanity case and currently a little wan leprechaun.

Every year I follow their fortunes, will them to win, ride the year's switchback with its highs and lows, and the seemingly inevitable net result now of a low high. Which in a way is the worst kind of result as it's all too clear what they could do, what they could be again. But where do you find another Ferguson?

And why can't I stop supporting them? Why am I worn to a frazzle, now the season's all over, with the feeling I've been beating my head against a wall? Indeed when they were doing quite badly early on this season someone told me a number of United fans had started self-harming and for a moment I believed him. More to the point, why do so many worldwide dream the United dream? This bunch of timid ditherers, these goldfish on their elephantine salaries, why don't we just let them go their ways, get lost in midfield, drift off the mental page?

It's a mystery. Maybe in part to support a team is for the very frustration it causes. One can rant and rave, hurl insults and soft slippers at the television, become an armchair manager of these pound signs in human form, one can fume and be unfair. Or one can watch and despair over one's "charges" as they evolve, rather as a long-serving teacher at a school, except that one does so with a complete lack of responsibility. Maybe, in the end, that's why one supports a team. To be gloriously irresponsible.

The train set in the attic
May 28th 2021

A dead ringer for the Mekon, Dan Dare's arch-adversary in the Eagle comic of the '50s, Dominic Cummings set out to blast the enemy to pieces and remodel Britain. A long essay of star-studded brilliance he wrote for Michael Gove as his advisor at the Department of Education says it all. It's a state-of-the-art summary of key points in what might be called a genius curriculum, which many may take up but only a Mekon can ever truly be master of. The underlying vanity emerges time and again in scornful language directed towards his inferiors – such as top civil servants – and one cannot help seeing a classic case of egomania in which practical results count for little or nothing beside a need simply to flaunt an idea of himself. To flourish to the world the credentials of the top banana.

The ridiculous thing is that he so nearly was that. He rose without trace (as Kitty Muggeridge said of David Frost) to become a kind of supremo without portfolio, second in organisational power only to a Prime Minster none too keen on the minutiae of the day-to-day. Then the traces showed only too clearly in his vilely dismissive language, his infantile dress code, his blatant dishonesty on breaking the Covid rules . . . and now the yah-boo aura to his testimony on the handling of the pandemic. What is amazing is that someone so evidently lacking in personal maturity should have been given such scope.

It's the train set in the attic complex that new leaders are subject to. Only Reagan, of recent leaders in the US or the UK, has had the sense to take his time about things, to do as little as possible until something required doing. In other words to let change evolve, with a tweak or prod here and there, and not to frenetically re-map, to give society a new lay-out, to make everything whizz and sparkle in spectacular fashion, as if the whole shebang could be created anew. Perhaps the Prime Minster has been cured of his Mr Toad-like predilection for charging ahead regardless, which Cummings so ably gave a veneer of reality to, and is learning a truer regard: for people, for process, for the patience with which so many are trying to make a difference.

I find it interesting that after graduating from Oxford Cummings spent three years in Russia. He's certainly revolutionary in outlook, totalitarian in delivery style, a man with a cause if there ever was one. I doubt there's anything in it but one wonders . . . Meanwhile one must hope that while a shake-up can at times be what is needed, the Prime Minister is less keen on the idea of tinkering with the flashing lights of a new system, and more inclined to emerge from the attic of invention, where he has been trying to defy gravity at altitude . . . and to come down to earth.

Leaf burst
May 30th 2021

This time, this time
let us applaud it
in spirit, too,
as we too bud-break
and shed the scales
of a dark time.
The walls teeter
of a protective prison,
the gates thrust open,
and over the land
what dance is this?
Never have I looked
at the light of an elm
as if I too
were of that element,
never have I touched
the midrib of a leaf
and drawn a fine

light affirmation
from that slight shape
with its sawtooth margin,
never before
have I felt so open
in the summer air,
or been so grounded
in the land's greening.
This time, this time
of leaf burst, let us
look to our freedoms
with a light touch
and careful hand,
with the wit to know
of the modesty
of the give-and-take
at the heart of Nature.

Techers
June 2nd 2021

TECHERS

I am not usually obstanat but I protest to being like a monkey in a cage I Hate losing My P.E. but I can not stand Having to Writ a an S.A. Im fed up and can not stand any mor

Another fragment from the distant past, 1967, my first year of teaching. It's still there somewhere in my mind, a tiny voice of a matchless personal dignity: what can one do? In an ideal world one would offer this bloke a drink and say how sorry one was. But it aint ideal.

Another lad in the same lesson (I imagine they were aged 11 or 12) wrote about one of his friends.

ANDREW

Andrew is a theif and he smokes and my mum told me not to play with him but I still do. Andrews hobbies are robbing Nicking and theifing. His father was a gangster you might have seen him on the pictures his name is Alcopne His Mother was also a gangster her name was Bonnie Parker and his brother was Jack the ripper he was so clever that the police could not catch me. And his grandmother was machine gun Lil.

I don't think I ever knew who Andrew was but he was certainly a fellow worth identifying with. An epic crew, a family for the ages. I must have told the class to write an essay about somebody they knew, an ill-advised topic no doubt. In any case it brings it all back, that first chaotic year, that sense of being driven backward by the tide, of just about keeping one's head clear of the wreckage, of finding one's feet occasionally on a sandbank and learning what a holiday really was.

But I also learnt something about children, which maybe was the first step to becoming a "techer" and not entirely and utterly – as I was then for the opening writer – a pariah, beyond the pale. In the current discussion of ways to make up educational ground lost in the pandemic the air is laced with a kind of shocked pound-sign earnestness. But basically all that matters is that children don't mind too much being in your class. It's half the battle. Which means – let techers be techers.

I once knew an art teacher at a boys' secondary school who couldn't understand how one of his colleagues, who taught Maths, achieved the terrific results he did, especially considering the mad torrents of noise from his classroom. So my friend crept along the corridor one lesson till he was outside that classroom, with his head below the level of the window in the door. Peering up he saw it all. The blackboard was divided into two halves, on the left a chalk drawing of a beautiful woman's face with luscious red lips, on the right her backside. When a boy solved a problem correctly he was called to the board and indicated to kiss the lips on the left. If wrong he had no choice but to similarly salute the drawing on the right. The boys learnt Maths.

In my career I may not have consistently offended against the shibboleths of political correctness as much as did this teacher, but I did not exactly tick the right boxes (and that's another story). All I would say to the powers that be, in a profession to do with individuals, is – don't stamp on individuality. Let techers be techers.

Techers
June 4th 2021

(continued) Of course in the current situation money matters and an extra fillip is needed. But a lot can be done with an additional catch-up grant of £1.4 billion and to throw ten times that amount at the problem, as the recovery task force has demanded, is quite possibly to throw half down the drain. Spending per pupil has more or less tripled in my teaching lifetime and academic standards have gone down, even as children may be better looked after now as people at school. A ridiculous amount is poured into the apparatus not of teaching, but of proving that teaching is going on. The apparatus of teaching is no more or less than the people who do it. The best approach is to hand out more as may be needed after it is shown the first hand-out has by and large been put to good use.

Box-ticking. The plague of the times. Returning to the UK after a sojourn in India I found myself teaching in the private system and at one point had a lesson assessed by a deputy head. Of the 25 or so boxes to tick I received a failing cross in 19. I had tried to teach a good lesson but had decided not to read the endless detail to do with a two-dimensional procedure of lesson planning, details of syllabus recording in pupils' folders and goodness knows what else, but to proceed as I always did. Coincidentally, in the same time frame (it might have been one or two days before or after the inspection), there was a parents' evening for that year. The observed lesson was with a bottom set of only nine pupils, all with significant developmental problems in the cosmos of mind and personality. One or two parents turned up for each child; and of the nine families, I was told by five (pupils were not present) that I had made a difference to their child's life. (It may or may not have been a coincidence that the deputy head had recently sent out a memo to all staff to abandon the use of forenames when writing a child's report. I think it was to avoid mis-spellings. I had rebutted this with respect but fairly forcefully and my view had been taken by the management team as a whole.)

Before leaving for India I had been a head of department for over twenty years, a senior teacher and on the school management team for fifteen, and while there were failures along the way, I knew what I was doing. I recount the anecdote above to illustrate a slip, an error in our ways regarding the encouragement of good teaching practice. We have to take the robot out of the human and not the reverse.

Pupils must be protected from wild personalities who can do harm in a number of ways. But just as each of his or her charges has something a little maverick or offbeat about them so in a way does a good teacher. If individuality is recognised – and children always know when it is – the dynamic of humour and change is taken on board, and the mind is allowed not only to find its way but to spring forward. There's little hope for it but the beginnings of a re-set could be here, if the £1.4 billion were used absolutely not for more training for teachers, nor for anything but allowing them to get on with the job as they see fit, with sensible but not over-elaborate checks. Let teachers be "techers".

Tantum religio…
June 6th 2021

Tantum religio potuit suadere malorum.

'Religion has talked so many into such evil.'

A Roman poet-scientist of the first century BC, Lucretius makes a point that can never be forgotten. For illustration he takes the sacrifice of Iphigenia. His 'religio' is not quite our 'religion' but close enough in this case for purpose. The following points are not his.

The space a religious belief occupies in a person's being is bound to include a pocket of delirium. This can be anything from a minute self-contained area of the mind or psyche, always kept well in check, to an enveloping singularity of mind-space in which any hope of a balance of sanity is lost.

A speck of that delirium is to be found in the idea – a mistake in the airwaves – that a formulated sound has value in itself. That to pronounce a name of God can alter things.

From that there's a direct connection to all the hurt and the hate, the horror and the cruelty, that will forever be a legacy of religious belief.

A state religion – any totalitarian ideology – is no different. Except that the means used has all the resources of the land at its disposal, to compel people to love – whomever it may be – from *within*. 'He loved Big

Brother' – the last sentence of '1984' – Orwell was right.

Whether or not they are overrun in this way by the machinery of state, because of a volatile bubble in the mind where it touches on the personality it is interlocked with, the capacity of people for religious belief has for long been made use of as the most terrifying instrument of manipulation the world has known.

How is it then that the religious world is the most beautiful creation of humans?

A Wild Flower
June 8th 2021

A Wild Flower

To see a World in a Grain of Sand
And a Heaven in a Wild Flower
Hold Infinity in the palm of your hand
And Eternity in an hour

Blake was a religious man and his own man. The opening verse of 'Auguries of Innocence', while it introduces a series of precepts of a fierce tenderness and beauty, also stands on its own. It is a glimpse of the future. There is a gift of seeing, and being, that can visit anyone – with or without the God-word.

The poem is the catechism of a spiritual leader who uses some of the formalities of religion in his own way – but as story. Just as 'a Heaven' above is devoid of literalist fantasies, a bearded patriarch, winged angels and so on, so later the word 'God' is at once indicative of all the goodness and love there is, and no more than a light knot in a piece of string to hold a parcel together.

Blake himself was a man of his time, though one of the most far-seeing and original, at least in this part of the world. In several of his poems he was besieged by his own God-ramblings. In this one he would have said he meant 'Heaven', 'Last Judgement', 'divine' and 'God' literally. This is because we have not yet learned the rational structure of the bridge that takes us from prose to poetry and back. Since rationality descended upon the world we have been looking for a way to talk about this. It's there to be found and when it is, there's a chance for religion to begin to lose its new-found literalism and eventually to be taken out of the great power game. And something most interesting might come in its place.

There is something like a radiance of being, and one might almost say a justification, where the power of a divine hand can be felt. This is neither within nor without so much as "inwith". Yet the word 'divine' is no more than a shorthand. Wonder is at its core; and a need for an explanation that cannot be (as yet); and a sense of ourselves with our 'discourse of reason', 'looking before and after' (as Hamlet has it) – together with the sense of goodness itself – such as to indicate our being here for a purpose, to be of service. All this requires gathering up, storing, communicating, honouring.

To capture it there is a shimmering spider's-web of story which we tend now to construct in heavy strands of gold. Eventually – unless religion can accommodate itself to its starting-point, something fine in both senses of the word – it will continue to stomp about the stable till the stable falls down. Maybe then it will rebuild in some corner or other – and hold.

These stories are the most beautiful thing there is. And taken in opposition to one another they are the most dangerous.

Unholy Places
June 9th 2021

In 1992 a large Hindu mob tore down the nearly 500-year-old Babri Masjid mosque in Ayodhya in northern India. Legend had it that it was the birth-place of the man-god Rama, an avatar of the Hindu god Vishnu, and that a temple to Rama had once stood there. 2000 died in riots all over the subcontinent.

The government of Narendra Modi has actively pursued a policy of 'hindutva', an aggressive pursuit of the Hindu identity at the cost of others. It is no accident that the Supreme Court of India recently gave the go-ahead for a temple to Rama to be constructed on the Babri Masjid spot, with no space now allocated for a new mosque also at the site (though an earlier court decision had granted it).

Thus is India losing something of its ecumenical touch, by which despite a terrifying cross-slaughter of Hindus and Muslims following the creation of Pakistan, the two religions have managed to exist side by side in India for a fair time since, in a certain neighbourliness if not in perfect harmony. Yet I cannot believe Hinduism is in any danger at all of losing its distinguishing mark, an innate appreciation of the need for a non-literalist approach in religious matters. To put it differently, Rama is stronger than Narendra Modi.

But there are many such disputed places and all have a history of horror. Perhaps one of the most catastrophic in terms of world history is the rock in Jerusalem on which, on the one hand, God ordered Abraham to kill his son Isaac and then let him off; and from which, on the other, Muhammad ascended to the heavens. Given our tendency to attach a numinosity to a physical place (which in its exclusive and aggressive form it is time we grew out of), what is the way forward?

After 9/11 I hoped, forlornly, that Ground Zero might be re-built to house a church, a synagogue and a mosque. I was delighted to see recently that the foundation-stone had been laid for the House of One, an initiative in Berlin that will allow the three faiths to conduct their services in separate houses of worship beneath one overall roof, which will also oversee a common area for meeting.

Is it not something for the horror-house of the world to take note of?

Uncle Simek
June 12th 2021

A few years ago I received a bequest from someone I had never heard of. Simek Piaster was born in Warsaw in 1910 and was the only survivor from his family of the Nazi terrors of the Second World War. He managed to escape to the USSR, and from there via a camp in Italy to Australia, where he lived till in his mid-eighties he emigrated to Israel. He never married and was always seeking to establish contact with various far-flung members of the family he had lost. When he died in 2006 he left instructions for an apartment he owned in Israel to be sold and the proceeds to go to such family members as could be traced. He knew of my mother's elder brother but not of her (or me and my half-brother). She had lost contact with most of her family also and had known nothing of him.

In Israel he completed forms to do with the disappearance of his father and his mother, last heard of some fifty years previously when they had either been disposed of in the Warsaw Ghetto or taken from there to the Treblinka extermination camp. In the form he filled out for his mother (above), under 'Victim's Profession' he writes, 'House Wife and <u>Good</u> Mother'.

The underlined word says all the world to me.

From a couple of letters he wrote to relatives when he moved to Israel he appears to have been an anxious, sweet old man. He is clearly a goodhearted, energetic, caring person to whom family meant everything, and little family had he had. He fumes at the temerity of the Arabs whose claim on Jerusalem is a mere 1300 years old, compared with that of the Jews which goes back 3000.

Who am I to comment on anyone's views who has been through such an experience? As with the trauma at India's partition, still endured by millions, so in the next year the creation of Israel blasted deep into the rockface of history, present and future, for millions on both sides. And so in countless ethno-volcanic upheavals elsewhere.

It is trauma that we must learn to appreciate and find a way to respond to, on the opposed sides of every conflict.

Earlier in my life I had endured a minuscule trauma of my own. Born a Jew (on both sides) I was adopted at a very young age into a Gentile family where I was not at home. Meeting both natural parents in my late teens was a great stroke of fortune and remained so till their deaths and will stay so till I die. Yet I had a false re-introduction to a Jewish being I could at once locate in myself all too clearly and yet not at all. Culturally different I seemed to breathe a different air, not so much from my parents as from the world of certain cousins I met at the same time who did and did not welcome me. I proceeded with something unresolved at core. Nothing could be more trivial, in contrast to my uncle's deprivation, all that he went through. And yet when I heard from him post mortem and saw a word he had written and underlined on a form, I understood something and was eased at heart.

Thankyou Uncle Simek for my legacy.

Somewhere beyond a threshold
June 13th 2021

If you sit for a time on a seat near a colony of shaped stone, and let the world pass you by, something can seem to occupy the stillness. The stirrings of something. It doesn't take long before they're nearer than they were, these busy people with their silent footfall, their faces turned away or not quite visible, getting on with their lives. Can they see me? I get up and stroll slowly, slowly among them, but they are not here, they are the other side of something, somewhere beyond a threshold. Messages are everywhere, names, dates and family roles, some with good words for their going, but they don't see them, those notice-boards are for us, for me, for a time and times after. Theirs is a street of other times, other voices, it is not the same, not the same seeing, not the same knowing. Do they see each other? It is not the same, nor is it the same going, but something is stirring. A to-ing and fro-ing of strangers, of depths and distances, of families and times unknown. Yet all is as bright as the copper beech at the churchyard wall, the yellow roses bobbing slightly in the breeze, the tall nettles and grasses devouring a battered old grave at the back. I return to my bench in the shadows.

It is all in the mind. I sit alone in a garden of rest. And yet, while it may take my presence to make it so, no-one can tell me this is not a living meeting-place, with a current of being as sudden and as strong as any down the ages.

Little Gidding
June 15th 2021

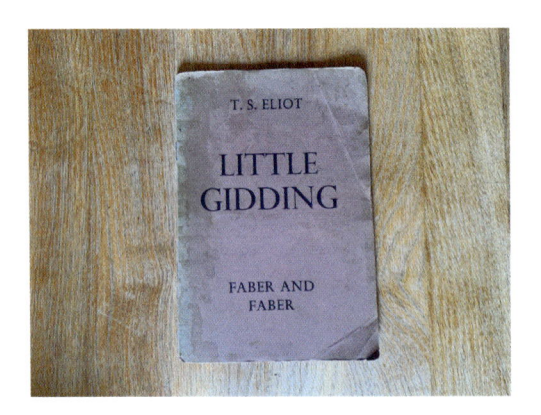

'**M**idwinter spring is its own season' begins T.S. Eliot's 'Little Gidding', the final canto of his meditative epiphany 'Four Quartets'. Like a great stained window the poem in its entirety casts light on who we are, in religio-existentialist terms, and will do for many an age. In hock to a certain intellectuality it sheds a narrow ray, but one perfectly loaded, as it has always appeared to me, with the full spectrum.

I'm at the remote Cambridgeshire village. In the church are a few wall-hangings, finely-stitched sampler-style, of quotations from Eliot, Nicholas Ferrar, an early-17th-century clergyman who founded a community at Little Gidding, and the poet and priest George Herbert who was Ferrar's friend. All round the church in the evening as I write are birds and dark trees and the solitary companionable aspect of Nature at its finest . . . I have nothing to say.

I came here to be here for a moment, taking a mini-break, as the lightening of the rules allows, from the dreary parochial lockdown that went on so long. On my way I realised the opening line to Eliot's final section (above) can be taken to speak for this very time of emergence from the plague. It has its own character, balanced 'between pole and tropic' as the poem has it. (Never mind we're almost at midsummer day.)

I hope Eliot's shade will forgive me if I congratulate Ol' Possum for an unintentional deepening of the status of a certain kind of economist or game theorist. The term 'zero sum' was first used in 1944 yet here he is, in a poem first published in 1942, looking out from the 'midwinter spring' of the spirit to ask, 'Where is the summer, the unimaginable / Zero summer?'

I should be banned from commentary forthwith. But I did come here for a reason. I have a copy of the first edition of the Faber and Faber pamphlet. Inside it is inscribed by my father on gifting it to my mother, 'New Year 1943', at which point I was about three months from being born. They split up before my birth but it is a precious memento of a closeness. So I came out here to Little Gidding, with a wonderful poem in tow, and a few disjointed thoughts somewhere between the sacred and the profane, and here I sit for a moment at the centre of an inner web, with a visit made to God knows where . . .

Whiff-whaff
June 17th 2021

I'm bushed. Boshed. Bashed. An hour's table-tennis and I know I've been in a fight. But you should see the other guy.

He's my son, a competitive fellow. (See the GK crossword entry of Feb 18.) It was his first game for about eighteen months whereas I've managed to get a bit of practice in elsewhere. So a win is a win and I'll take it, especially against him. I thought I'd given up the *numero uno* position with grace, not that I've done anything with grace that I can remember. But now there's a chance of reclaiming it, I feel as if I'm standing for all the fathers there have ever been who have fought to maintain position, to delay the handing over the keys of the world to the elder son. To postpone the inevitable.

Table-tennis is an excellent form of adversarial physical immersion where you just hit a ball. The mental pummelling of mind-games is there too behind the scenes as one is always calculating surprise tactics, working on an opponent's momentary weakness – as it may be, his backhand defence – and above all, keeping an eye on oneself, holding form, driving out the unforced errors. All physical sport has this mental angle, all thought sport has an atavistic shadow of physical struggle. Even Scrabble.

But whiff-whaff, a fine name for the game (though properly without the second h), or gossima as it's been called, or more usually now ping-pong (though that too is starting to sound dated), as an intense and precise hurly-burly of flailing arms and instinctive blind reactions, is my body-mind sport of choice. Regarding the modern scoring method as an abomination, limiting successive serves as it does to two, when I play it's always in sequences of five, with twenty-one points the line to aim for instead of (horror) eleven. There will be those who see a political animus in my use of the name of the game the Prime Minister used as Mayor of London (when promoting the Olympic Games there). But there will be those who see a political animus in anything.

I'm a peaceful chap myself. I merely wish to lather the ping-pong ball to my opponent's destruction, to annihilate the enemy in a card-game, to blast a chess adversary off the edge of the board into the sea. Later today I shall be teaching a seven-year-old the elements of draughts, and I shall be delighted if he relishes capturing my pieces and begins to plan to do so. To pass on the intensity, the craft, the heartlessness to win – that's the meaning of life.

The first days
June 20th 2021

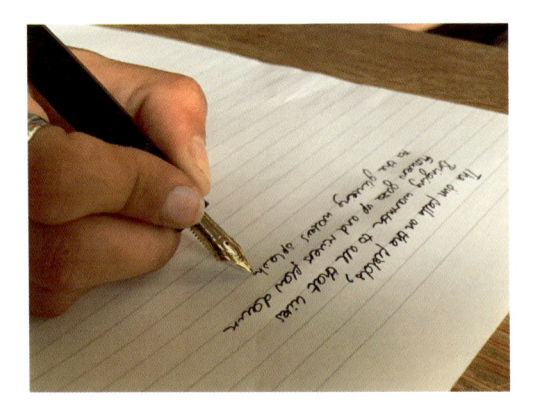

Why am I driven back a half-century, to what seem now like the first days of my adulthood, to revisit a batch of children and their poems? Perhaps it is by way of opening a door that must close soon. 'The first thing that happened to me was this: / I taught for a term in a girls' school' began a verse I wrote after my first spell as a teacher, a fill-in post at an Islington comprehensive. At two or three more schools in the early years of my career poetry of a remarkably high standard continued to drift in and land on my desk: a fact, something intricate, precious, lasting. Yet why it should have happened then in abundance, and rarely if at all later, is something I have never understood.

Sally Radcliffe was the least inhibited in character of all the young poets I encountered. A fourteen-year-old with a deft assurance in her writing and an inner ease, as it seemed, in the dodgem-car existence of the school's hurly-burly, I remember her entering the classroom more than once with arms held high, in a self-decree of victory. "Hi fans!" She was as bright as a sixpence, loved arguing, and wrote a number of brief war-sketches in verse that carried the shock of savage hurt and dying. (The Vietnam War was all over the air-waves.) My favourite poem of hers however is an altogether different exploration, the moment of a mind looking to the past.

THOUGHT

I retraced the steps of my tangled mind
to a twisted summer 10 miles ago
and recalled fragments of time
and periods of fathomless thought.
I rolled down the slippery slope of remembrance,
and, upon reaching the bottom,
discovered the bottom to be very far away,
lost in clouded memories,
misted by recent happenings.
Further I sank, and nearer the depths,
yet these seemed further away.
I slipped and skidded into traps,
and, deterred from my special quest,
saw a milky baby pat a green leaf,
and whisper Love to the sun.
And a far-away bee
softly droned in my ear
its honeyfied message
of nectar and pollen.
A small, dead flower
drifted in the streams of my thought,
losing the wrinkled-brown petals
one at a time.

A stone fell into my beautiful stream
and it drifted quietly
into a magic of far-far-away.
My mind raced on ahead of me,
leaving me lost in long-ago fields
where Lady Death beckoned
and all obeyed
and my thought, too, died
when she signalled to me.

Such poems came my way. If these web-log entries reflect a consciousness of any interest at all, when it is dead and gone, it will be in part due to a gift I was given, by a number of minds younger than mine, that somehow accompanied mine and seemed to know what it was up to. So I took my first steps as an adult, doing a job, and as it seems now, receiving some kind of a witness, as a poet newly on his way, no less than as a teacher, in the first days.

Halo-virus
June 22ⁿᵈ 2021

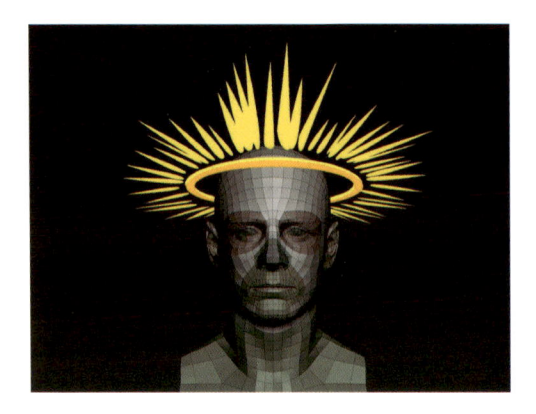

A virus seethes on Earth.

Its symptom is unmistakable.

It erupts in a blind and triumphalist anger.

This is the halo-virus.

Its R-number is stratospheric: but that is all to the good.

All who catch it become the soldiers of God.

With heavy breath and spittle they pronounce words of love.

They are the Holy Literalists.

They shall wipe humour from the face of the Earth.

Love is their hate and hate their love.

What is their aim?

With an army of anonymous trolls in the background, to dull and deaden the mind of society.

No statue of any human shall be allowed to stand: for it has feet of clay.

But there shall be statues of all in the Promised Land.

What things will they be, these statues?

The halo-virus is the deadliest plague-seed to visit the planet.

It knocks the coronavirus into a cocked hat.

One has brought death to millions.

The other is more savage, more subtle.

It targets the mind with a sleeping-sickness.

An alertness to others is starting to die.

We begin to forget our humanity.

Busker
June 24th 2021

We got him from an animal rescue centre, a lively-looking character about a year old who, we were told, was a tad nervous. Apparently he had been kept on a chain for many months in a yard, barking intermittently, till the neighbours called in the authorities. The first day he was with us the four of us sat down after lunch and resolved not to get up till we had a name. It took about two hours. Finally someone brought up the idea of a street musician and there it was: Busker.

The first weekend I got up early to add a bit of wire fencing to the garden wall as he was getting over it too easily into the adjoining garden. As I perched on a step-ladder I felt a lick on my cheek; he'd just cantered along the wall-top. I felt accepted.

He wasn't easy to train. I never achieved the obedience needed for his proper safety. The one whom he most listened to was our ten-year-old younger son, which pleased the lad mightily. Busker could be difficult: he often growled menacingly at bigger dogs as if spoiling for a fight. He got into one once with a huge animal who in a trice had him on his back with his neck threatened by a massive gaping jaw. I thought he was done for but the victor merely drew a tiny drop of blood from the throat, teaching him a lesson with an exact precision. He still played merry heaven for years.

He was acutely attuned to the sound of the letter d. This was because we would ask him, "Do you want to go for a walk?" which soon shortened into 'Do – ?" Then we saw he would begin to respond to any d that he heard in the words yattering on about him. He was a deeply loyal animal and tremendous fun.

In recent nights he's appeared in my dreams. Three or four times it's been the same thing in different contexts: he hasn't been fed for many days, I've neglected to buy him food, he's thinning away almost before my eyes. Why I can't get him the food I don't know but there's always some undramatic hold-up: I just don't seem to be doing it. In one dream he actually indicated the place on the shelf where the tin of dog-food should be, pointing his nose or even perhaps gesturing with his paw. There's a sadness about him he never had in life. Why should it be? What does he stand for in an inner register of something I haven't done, something I should have done? Yet even now I remember as if it were yesterday, that loping along the top of the wall unseen, and a sudden lick on the cheek.

The ball-game
June 27th 2021

We spend our lives running up against a hoarding, a larger-than-life advertisement that we shouldn't need. But we do.

Lives in the public eye. World-names, national names, A-listers of this screen or that. This profession or that, this sport or that. This news-maker or that.

And we bounce back into the real world, into our own private orbit. As the A-listers do. As the *galacticos* do, to take a footballing term and kick it aloft. The news-space superstars. Monarchs, geniuses, moguls, war-leaders, all the movers and shakers rebound to reality. The world-beaters are beaten at their own game by the more real private individual. Why more real? Simply because it's the person we all have in common.

There's a condition of experiencing, calculating, resting, keeping going. Immersion in a few deeply personal things, with some amount of that immersion in the world outside. Thinking: groping and being sure. Doing things, mostly straightforward, but there is always something in which one can fail or succeed. And one is always learning about the world, by direct experience.

But the banner-names festoon the mind. We are condemned to being turned this way and that by the headlines they make, to being flapped back and forth between them, to jumping to the imperious random gestures they make in the chance winds. To following in their fashion.

It's a game. We all play it, it's the only one in town, the wild rides between the public and private aspects of identity. And after a certain age, let's say eighteen, we are all flapping a bit of a banner ourselves.

We can't do without our hierarchies. And thence the blown-up images, the larger-than-life reflections of aspects of life along the common way. The never-ending summons to the public arena. The endless hall of advertisements that flip our minds this way and that.

It's a ball-game and the mind is the ball. If I think (or write) of a great personage, I shall try to remember the vertiginous malady of the line between private and public, the head-spinning journey one never stops making. The inevitable distortion of the picture.

And I shall know, without seeing it, of a condition I share with that personage, something more accurate and quiet than any game. Beneath the world of the separate mind, a dizzying distraction that must be, lies the corner-stone of all minds. There's a path for each along a common way.

Rabindranath
July 1ˢᵗ 2021

One day, I hope, a film will be made about the life of Rabindranath Tagore (1861-1941). Satyajit Ray, the Bengali film-maker, created a minor version but the cinematic splendour that might have been is not there. For various good reasons it is a modest depiction; but in my mind it is time for something more. 'Rabindranath' will span the nineteenth and twentieth centuries in India, a tremendous vision of a country and an individual travelling towards independence. In the latter case the point of the journey would be no more than lightly implicit and that only late on. If the film were truly successful it would leave everyone who saw it with a sense of the turbulent and magnificent richness of life – their life – and with just the shadow of a notion as to a direction within it. To the fore, however, would be – quite simply – a great life.

Tagore was an astonishingly gifted and prolific poet, and much besides. Several of his poems are about death, which is never to be feared, but to be seen as an act of completion. Death can be silent, a last guest to visit; it can be tenderly triumphant, a groom come to claim his bride. It is welcome, but never before its time. As creative a character in his life as I for one have come across, bar none in the annals of history, Tagore's relationship with the idea of his own death, to put it clumsily, did nothing to hinder the flow. Far from being inhibited by it, one might almost say his approach was one to allow his gifts to go on giving, to find room always to develop, in the light of a joyful surrender at the end.

As well as being an artist on many fronts he was an innovatory force in the everyday culture of his time; and if not a politician in the conventional sense he was certainly a figure on the national scene to be reckoned with. He may come to be seen as the leader of a social-political movement before its time. A visionary, a man of action, a wordsmith for whom the river-shape of a poem seemed to emerge as if it were the most natural and refreshing thing in the world, in his time he had a world-presence. Who he was tends to be obscured by what he did. It is hard to step back, to see the man at core, to consider quite what it is that characterises him, and that even makes one ready to follow him, as it were. His life had many setbacks and probably some wrong turnings. But I think it is for his perspective that at heart I call myself a Tagorean.

Rabindranath
July 3rd 2021

(continued) Who he was, what he did. One is blindsided by the latter. It's as well to get it out of the way, to continue to be able to see him as an ordinary person, as ordinary as oneself.

Rabindranath's poetry is unequalled in lyric scope and variety. His novels, short stories, dramas of prose and verse and dance, and his penetrating essays on a vast array of topics, are all informed by the springs of a great poetic mind. His more than two thousand songs form a unique branch of Indian music. They are among his finest poetry. In later life he turned his hand to painting and is seen as one of those who took Indian art into the modern world.

He was a social reformer of particular import. On the educational campus, at the rural town's developmental centres, in the farmer's field, he brought in new ideas that at once prompted co-operation with the outside world, and led to a defining measure of independence from within. So it was with a lifetime of effort to encourage a generous and practical outlook on the part of his country, as she tore herself away from a subaltern political status and reached for the reins of self-government. Nor did his efforts stop at his country's borders.

'The Realisation of Life, 'Personality' and 'Nationalism' were themes of lecture tours he undertook in the USA and Japan. Perhaps the most-travelled person on the globe in his time, he met world leaders, renowned intellectuals (there is a famous conversation with Einstein), and many others. A Nobel laureate (in literature), known far and wide as a speaker and humanist, he touched a nerve in all he said and did and wrote. And in all he said and did and wrote he was a poet.

'Poetry' literally is a making. An old word for a poet is a 'maker' (or Scots 'makar'). The current of words, that seeps through one's fingers as a poet, has the threads of a vision in it and the poet's grasp. So Tagore saw life as it was with a hint of it as it could be.

And so the film I have in mind – that glorious dream – in the midst of a rampageous tapestry of a country and a world at a time of great array and change, would present an ordinary man beset by the wind of love and change and error and hurt. And through it all and despite it all – a man at one with himself.

Rabindranath
July 5th 2021

(continued) His life was pierced by a searing ray of tragedy and love. Kadambari was the girl-bride of a much older brother of his, Jyotirindranath, and about two years older than Rabindranath. They grew up together. In a Bengali household a younger brother-in-law is sometimes afforded a position of especial tenderness; and without doubt the two young adults shared an intimacy of the mind and heart that the poet treasured all his days. At the age of 22 a marriage was arranged for him; following tradition Kadambari helped to find the bride; soon after the wedding she killed herself. Rabindranath's deep love for her became the inspiration of his poetry. He was never explicit: a departed lover appears at moments in several poems and one or two notable passages of prose; here and there he acknowledges his debt to her as the wellspring of his poetic life; not once does he name her.

When I think what the Western media would have made of this, had Tagore been one of their own, and compare it with the sensitiveness of his countrymen on the issue, I am glad for his sake he was not born here. It has not been explored, very little speculated on: it is as if the characters are respected as living people. (Not that that means much in the West.) The nature of their friendship is of no concern. Whether Kadambari is the mysterious lady who reappears in his work, indescribably close and dear, I think maybe is: at any rate it does not seem wrong to suggest it here. There is no proof, but any number of pointers; and over the rest of his life it is as if in a private meeting he remained in touch with her, staying within the bounds of decorum; but not forgetting her, and what he had been to her and she to him.

His own wife died after nineteen years of an affectionate marriage. He did not re-marry. Two of his five children died soon after, each aged a little over ten years old. Another daughter was to die in her early thirties. His mother had passed away when he was thirteen. He lived on, unafraid of death, but more, as if privileged by the union to come, while living a life that is as far removed from a "death-wish" as is to be imagined. My film would show a few of the meetings of two dream-beings, Rabindranath and Kadambari, inexpressibly close and far, in their private world.

Tagore and Gandhi
July 8th 2021

On the public level Rabindranath was at the spear-tip of the force of change. He conducted an almost violent debate with Mohandas Gandhi in articles published up and down India on the outlook to be fostered, as the impetus gathered and drove towards Independence. With the greatest respect, for the last thing either could do was to advance an argument *ad hominem*, they tore chunks out of each other.

Gandhi was a political leader who could make things happen on the map. Tagore was someone who could scent the direction of things and warn, advise, cry out; he could also intervene to direct effect at times, such as when he renounced his knighthood (awarded by the British) after the massacre of hundreds at Jallianwala Bagh in 1919. Both men had essentially the same free India in mind but Gandhi's way ahead was always in hock, somehow, to a furious purity of intent. Yet while Tagore was the more practical visionary, Gandhi actually was able – such was his charisma, his sacrifice and force – to achieve a glimmer in his country and beyond of a more harmonious world-existence.

They disagreed on the caste system – while ready to die in protest against the practice and very concept of untouchability, Gandhi saw value in a son's profession always following that of his father (to avoid a damaging competitiveness). The Mahatma proselytised mightily for all to spin cotton for half an hour a day (to avoid reliance on foreign cloth); Tagore said he preferred to spin poems. And on the cause of the Bihar earthquake of 1934, while Tagore insisted we should not 'associate ethical principles with cosmic phenomena', Gandhi told everybody it was 'divine chastisement' for the sin of untouchability. Tagore was always aware of the narrowness of the tunnel of a blind religious ardour and the dangers it could bring. But he saw Gandhi truly as a Great Soul (Mahatma) who could and indeed was opening a door to a finer land. While Gandhi saw him as a Sentinel, called him Gurudev (beloved teacher), and valued his opinion at all times to the very depths of his being.

There was a great love between these two men, springing from a companionship of the mind. Together they were a tremendous if as it were a temporarily ill-fitting force: they bore the freedom of a nation on their shoulders that went far beyond the departure of the British. I have an idea the dialogue they initiated is yet to be played out, in their land and beyond. Their closeness was remarkable. At one point Gandhi began a fast unto death in jail in a desperate attempt to force the British government to withdraw a divisive policy. He wrote to Tagore, ' . . . I enter the fiery gate at noon. If you can bless the effort, I want it . . . I will yet prize your criticism, if your heart condemns my action . . .' After a few days, the prisoner now frighteningly weak and the whole of India holding its breath, the British government conceded the immediate point. Tagore had arrived (in poor health himself) with the Mahatma already in dire straits. He was able to welcome the poet and breathed to him, "Sing to me." Tagore sang one of his Bengali songs. Later that day the concession came through and Gandhi drank some orange juice and survived.

Tagore and Gandhi
July 9th 2021

(continued) Romain Rolland, a French writer and public figure of far-reaching humanist sympathies, knew and had the deepest regard for both men, and saw them in their difference. 'The controversy between Gandhi and Tagore, between two great minds, both moved by mutual admiration and esteem, but as fatally separated in their feeling as an apostle can be from a philosopher, a St Paul from a Plato, is important. For on the one side we have the spirit of religious faith and charity seeking to found a new humanity. On the other we have intelligence, free-born, serene and broad, seeking to unite the aspirations of all humanity in sympathy and understanding.' It may sound as if he prefers the philosopher but as a pacifist he was enormously moved – as was Tagore – by Gandhi's great battle on behalf of the principle of *Ahimsa* – non-violence. As much as anyone in two millennia Gandhi re-ignited the pacifist flame. But a clear head is needed with a clear soul. In a letter Rolland wrote to Tagore in 1923 he said 'the noble debate' between the two 'embraces the whole Earth, and the whole humanity joins in this august dispute.'

'Rabindranath' the film would carry in passing the opposition and deeper oneness of these two burning lights. It would also briefly picture a most unfeeling moment on the poet's part when he scathingly lambasted and rejected a remarkable book by a young Englishman, Edward

Thompson, who knew him, had read all his work to that point (1926) in the original Bengali, and published 'Rabindranath Tagore: Poet and Dramatist'. The book is marred by a very few tactless and ill-considered remarks (probably pointed out to Tagore by another English friend who resented the newcomer's temerity). In the main, as someone said at the time, it is a *hirak-ratna* – a diamond. Like the rest of us Tagore could snap, get things wrong.

But he was the greatest human being it has been my privilege to be near. He died two years before I was born but I have written poems about him, translated some of his books, and have been lightly yet almost continually refreshed by the closeness. He was a religious man, unlike myself: he once used the phrase, 'The play of love *(lila)* between God and the human soul', to describe a relationship I do not believe exists. But that does not matter. I may not believe in all his words but I believe in his outlook. We are all of us creative, we are all of us practical, we are all of us dreamers and doers, and a unity of action is to be found herein, a unity of being. This is why I am a Tagorean.

Ballad of the Tins
July 10th 2021

Man was made to warm things up (Martin Cruz Smith)

Of simple things I sing,
  fresh air, a quickening breeze,
a seagull's light grey wing,
  the far voice of the seas . . .
such dreams will drift and swing
  down with me to the grave –
with this grave-offering.
  Tins and a microwave.

Tins and their opening
  should be a thing of ease:
but the damned pull-up ring
  snaps off; nor can I seize
the lid with my whing-ding
  tin-opener, as I crave . . .
it's war. Still they're my thing,
  tins and a microwave.

Long bouts of counselling,
  I've had enough of these,
enough of suffering
  advice and recipes.
For me no apron-string,
  no stove-rags of a slave,
but the emblems of a king.
  Tins and a microwave.

Reader, what dodge can bring –
  admit it now, be brave –
the answer to everything?
  Tins and a microwave.

It's Italy on penalties . . .
July 12th 2021

The morning after, unremarkable, a little damp. Perhaps a tang of disappointment in the air. But along with that, for me at least, the faintest whiff of the safely-bubbled ozone of relief. We've been let off.

Had we won the land would at once have been a splendid place to live in and unbearable, suffused in a kind of red-and-white delirium of pride. Pictures of Gareth Southgate, the manager, would have been everywhere, engendering a new vision of a smiling but gritty authority. Harry Kane, the captain, would have been everyone's best mate, his slightly raffish, London-boy casual modesty jumping out at us from a thousand photographs and hoardings. The whole team would have been the new heroes, waving from a never-ending victory bus-ride the length and breadth of the country. Or so it seems to me, in the early morning after, savouring the freedom of defeat.

When we won the World Cup in 1966 I was working in a grocer's, the radio was on, and as we scored twice against Germany in extra time I remember charging up and down the floor kicking empty cardboard boxes at the walls. Nobody minded. It was a great moment. But in the following days and months the land's response to victory was hardly immoderate. A little political capital – imagine the bounce the government would have gone for now. A touch of jingoism – of the 'Two World Wars and one World Cup' variety – which is unpleasant in retrospect, if meant goodheartedly enough. But by and large everyone had other things to get on with. The aftermath was sane.

Would it have been now? One doesn't have to worry. One can indulge in armchair recrimination. My own view is that Southgate handled the substitutions badly, bringing on Rashford and Sancho with only a few seconds to find their feet before the game ended and the penalties began. They fluffed theirs, and the saddest thing about the game is not that England failed to win another major trophy even 55 years after the last (though the Euros is hardly the World Cup) – but that those lads will never forget their misses, nor will the country. One can also question Southgate's lack of any kind of vital response to the turn-around in the standard of play. Quite simply, England went from an assured and almost magical front foot in the first half to a leaden back foot in the second. Drastic action was required; it wasn't taken. Internally I had been screaming for Sancho and Rashford to appear for a full hour before they were finally ushered on, with no time at all to unwind on the pitch. The inexperienced Saka as fifth penalty-taker was also a curious choice. Did Southgate know at all what he was doing?

But that's football.

On the run
July 15th 2021

A photo was unearthed recently by a family member that took me back to my running days. So here I am leading a small pack – no doubt well down the field – in a half-marathon in 1984. I tend to think of myself as ageing at a respectably slow rate, but am somewhat discombobulated by this youngster who could clearly walk as fast as I can run now. There's nothing like the reality check of a 37-year time-warp.

It brings it back though, the bundling along, the trudging up hills, the trundling down them, travelling in the moment. The divorce from all other concerns. The short-term goal – to finish – refined only by – in a good time. (Winning or a high place was not an option.) The body hard at work yet of a piece. The being outside.

That year I ran my only marathon. All this time later it wraps itself around me, a python that tightened and tightened, till at last I was home free and let myself fall on the grass. The constriction thrown off I lay there liberated, inert, somewhere I have not been before or since. Eventually I returned to a shambling verisimilitude of the bipedal mode.

Many moments remain from that 26-mile canter but one stands out. A mile or so from the end yet another hill appeared and I found myself walking for the first time. Someone drew level, also dropped to a walk, and we started talking. "Helluva place to put a hill," I grunted. He replied with a drawn-out thought which I interrupted by simply running off. I count it as one of the rudest things I've done (and I have form as a social offender) – but I knew if I didn't, I'd be walking to the end. As it was I managed a time I can look back on without too much of a shudder.

Another memory is of a shorter conversation, about the shortest possible. Once I went for a training-run in the snow, which turned into a near-blizzard. I made out another runner coming towards me. As we passed we both shouted out, "You're mad!" and then were lost to each other. (Strangely, as I write I feel that moment too around me.)

A spell of long-distance running leaves its own memories. One I'd rather not have is of my children more than once over-hearing me, when I thought I was on my own, muttering something like, " . . . if I can get to that lamp-post in under 28 and Tibbet's Corner in 35 and go slap-bang down the hill then surely I can . . ." muffled sniggers. One gets obsessed. Once at a party I met two other runners and we simply talked times and training for two hours or so, all I'm sure hating ourselves for it yet unable to tear ourselves away and actually talk about something more interesting with someone more interesting . . .

Happy days.

Freedom Day
July 17ᵗʰ 2021

Two days before the "off", in delightful mid-July weather, it's as if the shackles are off already. Down by the sea group restrictions are off, in mid-town the opening-tape to trade is well and truly cut, everywhere the inhibitory mood is sunnily shed, just as the idea of any item of weather-resistant clothing has gone out of the window. Without any great drama the land's settling back into its drift of free association and free enterprise and everything will soon be back to normal.

As other lands settle back in their own way, over the next year or two, will there be any benefit at all to be derived from the commonalty of our experience? One would hope that at the very least virological science will progress more openly, internationally more than nationally. But it could so easily be less. China will be increasingly on the defensive regarding the origin of Covid-19. The race to make these damned viruses for the wrong reason is likely to hot up. In fact one imagines it already has. And still, projecting into the far future, a historian looking back on the time, is there nothing to be seen that was learnt by these 21st-century children with their outsize brains?

Who knows? Perhaps it will be no more than an implicit understanding of a shared coming-to-terms with loss. As the cracks in society are gradually papered over everywhere in terms of the unnatural breaks in education, general health provision, individual security and communal development, on the surface it will be merely more of the same. A gigantic wrestling-match of the currencies. The two superpowers repeating gambits of the Cold War but with the opponent of the free world now on a firmer foundation. Who knows what our historian will see? Perhaps it is for the artists of the world with their various materials to balance on the rim of the future and interpret the plague, to make us inter-conscious so that we can go forward from it. What a thought, that the frivolity of modern art may be jolted into something more telling.

And yet what kind of day will Monday be if we continue barely to raise an eyebrow at what's going on outside? As the Taliban provide their own answer to the finally outdated Great Game of the British and the West, will it be Freedom Day for the girls of Afghanistan?

A Rubbish Heap
July 20th 2021

Coming up to O levels, in a class I taught at the outset of my career, was a lad who seemed unable to step in time to the system and kept running across it. It announced itself negatively to him: one teacher would accuse him of rudeness, another of vanity, another of consistent lateness . . . they weren't wrong. But they were more wrong than right. He demanded to be told where each of the 24 marks had gone when he was awarded 26 out of 50 for an English essay; he insisted on trying to discuss 'Beowulf' with an English teacher who was embarrassed by her ignorance. He was late. He was also wonderful material to teach: quick with words and ideas, a boy with an unusual flair which would not be put down. Here is Paul Maltby on A Rubbish Heap.

While men sleep
From the fissures of the earth
Fire-brands leap, kindling torment.

As senses fade
Out of an Upheaval
Iconoclasts wade, worshipping evanescence.

Nothing to reap.
People, wan and empty,
This distorted Rubbish-heap.

When he handed it in he said the only poetry in it was the word 'wade'; but while idea and feeling may interlock there a second, the whole is a changing flame, a fantasy leaping into reality. In another lesson he produced something slower and in a way more startling.

STELLARPHOBES

Caught in the night!
We lay ourselves in earth,
We hide behind trees.
Paranoids go by in cars,
Hoot, and throw balloons at us.

Fear impedes our urination.
Then, lucky for me, hands cover my eyes
I'm being carried.
Next I'm safe in a car, I'll be home soon
And no longer exposed to the night.

I have an idea the title was his coinage and word-wise it may be the most memorable part of the poem. Yet the scene itself is successful, as the clip of a film. Paul did not find the going easy at school. All the young poets of this journal are pupils at comprehensives, at a time when such schools had not yet discovered the tricks and turns of the present academy system, which may be making a little headway on the long march to the promised land – a decent free education for all. But still and always – far too many pupils do no more than hobble through school.

It's an obstacle-course. If I had Paul's vision, I'd paint a picture in words of a rubbish-heap piled high with twitching adults of all ages, outside a school's gates. They survive, but a trauma survives with them.

Pet-Hates on Nightingales
July 22nd 2021

In the same class as Paul (see last entry) was a quite extraordinary young man – or at least young mind. At one point the following was handed in by one Adrian Gibson.

**PET-HATES ON NIGHTINGALES
(QUITE TRADITIONAL)**

The man you hate is like the woman you love, annoying.
Life is confusing, deaths are even better,
Fun is fanatic, death is even frightening –

Forty round a serpent bend, darkness ALL around
DEATH IS A SOUND.
Could it be so, flying off the road
Life's so exciting: 'I wonder where they're going?'

He's so annoying, Christ he should be
Donning his sabre soon behind your back (cutting).
Should he be crying: no he should be drowning.
Spitting all enigma
TRY TO IGNORE HIM.

God, she was so pretty,
Flying like a skylark, White is sole
Appreciation!

Sitting there so silent, crest upon a wing.
(She's really very pretty – and alone.)
What she does for dying, crying, lying,
Filing, – it's life.

'Twas once the very month of MAY.
HE, SO DAMNED BELIEING – he drowned,
Thank God. Life's so peaceful, so contentful.

But here we are today – it's fun – pity he's alive.

Though life is so confusing, so annoying,
But he's still there (I still laugh)
They'll never kill you yet (ONLY WITH LAUGHING!)

I could see him staged right now –
Professing of his life – misled fool.
Professing sheer compassionless, monotonous,
Distortionist disunion, and unkempt tolerance.

Adrian was unable to explain to me what this meant, what it was about, unable to pronounce on it at all. To him it was complete. Other poems he wrote were titled 'Through Glorious Specs Inverted', 'Life for Sale at the Market' and 'Natural and Artificial Dawn in Awakening'. I was at a loss as to how to help him. He was of a sunny disposition, and the contortions his writing went through seemed to do with a need to explore opposites and make an effect, rather than reflect a personality in any way at odds. He failed the English Language O level (but passed later), and occasionally down the years I have wondered where that mind went on to, what corners later it may or may not have turned. A line of his from the 'Natural and Artificial Dawn' poem has remained in my own mind: 'The quivering shores rattle without harmony.' I think with boys quite often the mind gets ahead of itself and out of kilter with its life-experience; while with girls there is more likely to be an even development. It's a difference of genders that can last life-long.

I can't remember now but it's just possible that I had gone through two famous poems with the class, Keats' 'Ode to a Nightingale' and Shelley's 'To a Skylark'. It's more than just possible that my teaching style – a kind of jabbering-on in a knowing way, on the look-out for inattention – had got under Adrian's skin. I rather hope so, looking at the superb conclusion of his poem. You can't win them all.

Time
July 26th 2021

Stephanie Martin was the same age as Paul and Adrian (see last two entries) but had been made to repeat what is now Year 10. I had no idea why. She was not academically minded but very much in touch with her feelings, and able to render them as an artist, as if in the full confidence of the palette of words. At first she wrote of melancholy. A poem called 'ALONE or TO BELONG' ended:

My grief is deep, I am a statue,
    Living, no existing in
a world full of nothingness.
    Please someone still my longing
    and unchain my passion to belong.

Later there was a poem of hate, which I lost. It started:

My soul is dead
    my mind a garden
planted with the evil flowers of my time.

It went on to attack people, just people, in a savage desperate way, and ended:

their minds are twisted
    their bodies are perverted.

When she handed it in she said I'd misunderstand it. Maybe I did, but I wish I had the rest of it. Though much of her poetry was 'dreamy', when she opened her eyes there was no stardust in them. In another poem, neither of hate nor longing, nor of anything except the individual and the universe, she wrote with extraordinary awareness.

TIME

Time stood still, the world spun off its axis.
My body went cold, Time took over.
I drifted from star to star, searching for my body.
I was a thing the Time had destroyed.

I saw the light circling round
first light then dark, then light then dark.
Time going on, the galaxy drifting on
but I was one thing destroyed by time.

I caught up with my thoughts, they were crazy
So I left them behind, I would start afresh
My thoughts were my own, to do with what I pleased
I was a thing that time had created.

My image was huge, my voice a whisper
a howling whisper, unseen but felt,
I know now, why I was destroyed.
  To be created into the wind, the howling wind.

Stephanie is where Paul and Adrian are not. The mind is as strong but it is not showy. It may be lost but it does not get ahead of itself. I am talking of a girl's mind, a woman's mind, which can give voice to things as they are, to the world of human perceptions, perhaps more directly (by and large) than a boy's or man's. Here an existentialist snapshot would not be out of place in any anthology of such. From my collection of poetry written by schoolchildren so long ago, and as it has found its way into this journal, I begin to see an evolutionary direction, no more than a straw in the wind. The real shift is towards the physically weaker sex becoming the mentally stronger (except, it may be, in the purely mechanical areas of thought). The balance that is needed for the understanding and forward movement of the human world is in their hands. But it will take time.

The Olympic flame
July 27th 2021

So many must have had the same thought. A frail shell, bristling with internecine rivalries, even as it emerges from the sweep of a plague-wind, puts on a world-wide show. The athletes in Tokyo perform in an extraordinary number of homes and public places across the globe. There is a warmth, for a couple of weeks, at the heart of the ramshackle business of who and what we are, a flame of driven excellence and effort, as if the fire of an ideal peeped through the miasmic wreckage of the strife and striving we are born and die with. As if a new day were possible. As if we could always, if we looked for it, find ourselves in the presence of a new way of doing things. Is it not in part what the Olympics are for? And this time we have the perfect image in the land of the rising sun.

Bleed, bleed, bleed. The same sun blinds our day as it always did. For two weeks there is a loyalty to tribe – and to something more. What we could be, what we could do. What we are, at heart, a skilled and loving people. Then the mirage of something different is wiped from the skies. It is as if the four-yearly reminder – a little late this time – had not been.

Bleed, bleed, bleed. The same old earth, the same old sun. What have we done with our inheritance? For two weeks there is a rivalry at once intense and unpernicious. Virtually everyone feels it. Then the abominable screams fill the stage again of power for power's sake, and of all the suffering born of it.

Bleed, bleed. For two weeks the Games, that great bowl lit against the odds from a world-travelling torch, transcends our frailty even as it captures it – this time perhaps as never before. It was so close to being cancelled, so many athletes have been disqualified by Covid-contact, there was such an outcry in Japan itself against the staging. But for a fortnight the country will have offered a testimony as to what can be done. And who knows, the very frailty and strength of the undertaking may this time leave a legacy of its own.

This is all too wordy. But so many must have had the same thought while waiting for this event, or recalling that, and feeling the impetus gather. A lightning-flicker of a holistic meaning, perhaps better not put into words at all. But it will keep the heart alive.

S.W.A.T.
July 29th 2021

It doesn't take long for the Special Weapons and Tactics unit of the Los Angeles Police Department to tamper with the heartstrings just a little. This screen-cop outfit that day after day (it seems) keeps the master criminal mind at bay in L.A. quickly becomes our ally, somehow, or we become its: so we do the good work together, all miraculously unscathed. Two questions in passing – why are the bad guys always such lousy shots? And why aren't females more often handed that evil-spider role, that Moriarty intelligence? Crime fiction has some way to go. Anyway this central SWAT team of a half-dozen or so quickly allow us into their back-yard of aspirations and failures, their triumphs and tragedies – even if they are too busy to take note of ours. And so we live their manic headlong life with them, almost one of the family.

The team is a family of its own. In action everyone has everyone's "six" (o'clock, their back) while at the same time living out a quite subtle interplay of meta-familial roles. Sibling-type rivalries, authority figures offering "tough love", the whole family web is there, the web we carry with us (however torn or broken) all our days, the web by which to a degree we understand the world. That the SWAT team is a family (and so survives) is an underlying motif that goes deep.

A pervading surface theme is the different perceptions of black and white people of the tensions so deeply lodged as to be almost embalmed in colour difference. At one point a desperately urgent discussion between the (black) leader of the group, and his (white) deputy who was in line for the job but denied it by a technicality, examines this theme at some length, while bullets flail around them. Normally training kicks in and they take cover but in this case there's no time even for that. Such impractical earnestness however is an anomaly and in general a light touch rules; and the black/white theme is handled as a result with a telling force. Another surface theme is simply that of leadership; and another, linked to that, is the path that has to be forged in every individual case by the strong woman.

The main theme, however, less explicit and more pervasive than any of these, and which hands SWAT its Oscar in a way, might be said to be the difficulty of good love. I am not at all sure this was a conscious thought in the minds of the film-makers. After all, in an ephemeral series chock-full of action and made above all for entertainment, we are hardly intended to listen to a sermon. Except that this particular aspect of reality, in some guise or other, is likely to enter every form of literature that lasts. And so something from my latest wild Netflix escapade will last for me.

Whether it's in a romantic context, or one between mother and son, or son and father (how often the American screen trembles with a father-son clashing of gears and at last an easing-forward); or whether the issue lies between cultural siblings or cultural opposites, what stays is the hard road to love.

At the Clifto
August 2nd 2021

At the Cliftonville pub in George St., cross-wording with my son (not as acrimonious as it looks or sounds, see entry Feb 18), a bill for two margherita pizzas, a pint of Stella and the same of blackcurrant and soda has just come to £13 something. It's ridiculous. Add to that the Wetherspoon pubs' policy of no muzak and the place is a haven for quiet souls.

Except that some people come here, it seems, to laugh. Screech screech. It should go the way of the muzak. Perhaps with everyone's instincts to follow instructions honed to fever-pitch by Covid, one might make and glue firmly to each table-top a warning: 'In the interests of limiting virus spread it is forbidden to laugh at this table. Vocal Cords. NHS. Save Lives.'

I reckon it might work. And the idea might be catching. There's too much laughter in the world anyway. Again and again I happen to turn on the television (Can one still say that? "Turn on"? It seems so dated) and there are three or four jackasses in a studio laughing their heads off. The word is, Get the viewers to laugh. Then they'll come back. People laugh at the flimsiest reason possible. They should be put in the stocks.

Back to cross-wording. I use the hyphen here to suggest the to-and-fro yatter between the generations, as we look up from the clues. We're both learning, he possibly more than me as he's more open, I think, to different points of view that may or may not confirm his thinking or develop it. Whereas I'm of the opinion I have little to learn.

The staff at the Clifto are rushed off their feet. Too many absentees. The "pingdemic" is playing havoc with staff everywhere. The country is still inching along nervously, the blind leading the blind. But it's still marvellous just to be able to walk in, drink, eat, talk, come to in the mornings, settle back in the evenings. A home from home.

Not every day, you understand. Sometimes – not that often – I have things to do. But what a moment it was when the old Clifto re-opened after the lock-out. Sitting there, that first Edenic morning, I was (in mind at least) an open, fresh-faced gent who was not only more than content to be alive but – perhaps a first in my adult life – more than content that others were too. For a day or two I didn't even mind the laughing.

At Lagwyne Cottage
August 4th 2021

'Lagwyne' or 'Low-lying Sepulchre' (with a short quick 'la' and 'gwyne' to rhyme with 'twine') survives in a number of place-names in a quiet area of Galloway in south-west Scotland. It is quiet yet time-charged: I have rarely, perhaps never felt a stretch of land pulsate with such a presence of the past. I am staying in Lagwyne Cottage, which is bordered on one side by a ragged defiant remnant of castle-wall. It is in fact the remains of a fortified manor built by the family of John Loudon McAdam, who invented what became known as the macadam method of road construction.

But beneath the roads and grasses of all the rural surface hereabouts it seems as if a world is being sifted. Far, far before any stabilising effect of modern engineering took hold, far before the Romans too administered an arterial touch to the surroundings, old structures have risen and fallen, there has been a coming and going, change has opened a way. The blind bluster of human intent is still to be heard, still to be felt in a time-echoing region such as this. It is near the surface.

Next to the cottage is a field with two burial mounds. The higher of these is likely to have given rise to the cottage name, where 'wyne' means 'sepulchre' and 'lag' a hollow or dip in the surrounding hills. I do not know if I overhear a connection as I walk about and between the mounds. But voices can be heard. Voices of machinery and great song and of one time tumbling into another. And voices of sadness.

We who live on the surface of things are attached to the past in a way we cannot see. The day of life is sifted like a dream in the night of death. Though there is no direct sequential day following there is a reason for such echoes, a reason why from place to place and time to time we can pick a few up. There is a high road to change and a low road, perhaps, that together can open a way.

At Lagwyne Cottage
August 7th 2021

THERE IS

there is there is

a whisper spreads to a field
of heads of wheatgrass

a rumour hides in the bursts
of reeds and rushes

it is it is

the bracken confers, the thistles nod

a huddle of beeches at the side
come to a view, spectators both and judges
note the reports, accept the proposition

it is

almost not there, I skirt a burial mound
to enter a room of light *what is it what is it*

a chamber of the mind and sky and field

an in and out, a more-than-life, an instant
caught and gone, and all-at-once confirmed
as a meadow pipit starts from beneath my feet

there is

there is

there is

Old and new
August 10th 2021

What was it when I went to India for the first time in the summer of 1990 that got under my skin, into my bloodstream, and took me back there for a stay of twelve years? Still now that first pinprick of an awareness of something that, if I stayed, was probably going to engage me at a deep level, replays itself; and still I can say nothing intelligible about what I learnt. Only that I began to learn it a little.

It was the contrast with what I was used to that alerted me. The mix of old and new was different. At the time, on that first visit, I heard it as a kind of sound, almost a bell-note. I scarcely thought about it again, all the years I was there, and have scarcely thought about it since. If I do now, it is as something more active than a sound, more a tingle in the blood. But what was it I was alerted to? What is it I am no more than alerted to now, if at a more vibrant level? Perhaps it is the start of a perception that arrives in any case, whether one travels or stays still, part of the apparel of age. I can only speak for myself. For me its arrival is something to do with my own in a land where it can seem that nothing is ever forgotten, and what might be dramatic change elsewhere is no more than a puff of wind.

I saw a scene from the Mahabharata sculpted on the side of an ancient temple for those who could not read. (As a church window or a religious painting in the West may also have come to pass.) I was shown headlines in a newspaper where the names of characters from the same epic from the dawn of literacy were used as personality-tags for modern politicians. (And recently in the UK I taught a child named Darius after the Persian king of kings.) I see that it is nothing to do with where I went. Yet where I went helped me to see it.

And that mighty bell-note of India still sounds as, ageing now, I am taken into the living stream. That fortunate stay, which gave me my send-off from youth, in this way and that also let me glimpse an inkling of a state of flux at the core, a dissolving unity, where my own bloodstream is headed. It is only now that I can begin to give it words.

At the end of a lane leading up to a cottage I stayed in recently (see last two entries) is an old beech tree-stump that's given up the ghost, except for a new young rowan rising out of it. It's an economical image, and as effective a statement as the material world may have to offer, of the old and the new.

Durga
August 13th 2021

Since leaving India I have missed Durga. Kali is ever-present, in the perfect storm of her being, able to manifest a mighty power merely by the stories about her. She and Durga (with others) are alter egos of the female divine, charged with its different faces so to speak, wives of Shiva (see entries pages 58-61), and both one and the same and altogether different. In the Hindu pantheon aspects of personality are distributed and individuality heightened, in my scant experience, like nowhere else on Earth. It is so too for the male. The shifting element at the core of all things is known.

In Kolkata I knew Durga. Her ten-day festival in the autumn is a colossal panorama of human fortunes mirrored in the divine, a riot of ease and a springing rain of grief, a time when one knows the community and the community knows one, when 'knows' means simply 'is of', when the tribe has no boundaries. The city roars. As does every square metre of every village in West Bengal. There is a possession of people by the land and the land by its people; but it is time to give the barest indication of the song of existence the festival is.

For six days Durga is on her way back home. Leaving her husband Shiva back in their Himalayan abode but taking her four children with her (gods and goddesses all), she is visiting the house of her childhood.

She is any Indian woman who has left home to get married and from time to time comes back. Pandals or temporary temples are put up and painted screens are set inside bearing images of the mother goddess and her remarkable brood. There is a tremendous buzz of expectation before the arrival which leads into an extraordinary four-day drama of the open. Days seven, eight, nine and (incontrovertibly) ten mark the visit and the start of the return. These are the "great days".

The details are too many. But in those last few days city and country have been awake. The reflection of the journey of each individual has passed over street and home. A spark of life, with some of its main consequences, has been struck and is now to fade, not to die but to be renewed. After being there for Durga's festival a couple of times, at the start of my stay, I seemed to know her all year round; and at the ten-day *puja* itself I felt she knew me. If I return at that time I imagine the same will happen. She is my India. Wherever I am I know Shiva all the time, as I know Kali. But I miss Durga.

A new game
August 16th 2021

It could go one way or the other. Now in solitary control of Afghanistan, have the Taliban an opportunity to win friends?

Twenty years ago they lost control with a name in the global annals of shame. Their terrible treatment of vast numbers of Afghan civilians and especially women, their destruction of land and homes and of priceless relics of the past (the Bamiyan statues of the Buddha), their rigid ban on some of the most joyous forms of artistic expression, their ferocious and anachronistic absolutism as to how society is to function . . . these are not grounds for hope. Yet grounds there are. Suddenly the West is out of the way. After not far off two hundred years of surviving a death-game of outside presences, as it must seem, the country has the glimmering of a chance to get its own act together. The Pashtun culture is protective and strong. Certainly it would treasure the respect of the world. How can we speak to that?

It is very much a question of tone. If we are not at war with a country then dialogue is the way forward. But what sort of dialogue? Nations are lining up to refuse official recognition to the new régime. But to offer a temporary recognition, conditional upon a slight relaxation in the interpretation of *sharia* or Islamic law, might be more productive and lead on to a less guarded stance. One cannot expect the wheels to turn at all, let alone at any other than a blindingly slow pace. Yet a block or two can be shifted.

Imagine if our Prime Minister, a lover of poetry, began an international address by reciting a Pashto *ghazal*, a poem of love and separation in musically aligned couplets. He would have the autocue to hand and it would not take him forever to learn the main nuances of pronunciation beforehand. But it might be remembered forever. Simple things, little things, can make giant headway. And what harm would be done?

Perhaps the original question should be turned round. Does the West have an opportunity to win friends? Or will we be too intent on hammering home our own unmistakable message to stop it all going the wrong way?

Ballad of the Books
August 19th 2021

BALLAD OF THE BOOKS

They gather on my shelves like crows
   in mocking, gleeful disarray,
and where they come from no-one knows.
   At times I make some go away
but more return. These dreadful rows
   at which I yell profanity –
they are my friends, they are my foes,
   they are my curse, my sanity.

Voluminous dust-specks drift, to close
   upon a private realm, where they
accumulate like waves, like snows,
   unsortable and all astray . . .
yet where they land up a sun glows.
   They are my vice, my vanity,
they are my friends, they are my foes,
   they are my curse, my sanity.

The shelves sing a raucous song. Time goes
  to bits, space clutters. In dismay
I know the richest things are those
  which wreck our ease, turn night to day.
These jewels of poetry and prose,
  these seed-beds of humanity,
they are my friends, they are my foes,
  they are my curse, my sanity.

Reader of same, do you suppose
  they chuckle at our inanity?
They are our friends, they are our foes,
  they are our curse, our sanity.

If we are free
August 21ˢᵗ 2021

. . . of the gaping scythe of Covid . . . then *Hallelujah!*

Since I stood on Earth
a hundred thousand years ago, or a minute

I have paused to listen to a medley of notes on the air
to birds and insects and animal calls, to whispers
of men and women at love, to children at song

I have heard the scorching argument of the sky
deliver a death-blow, and as peace breaks out
I have heard the new air in its silences

from the sea's stones I have heard the waves' discussion
from grass I have listened to the high mad dances
of the singing freedom of a sack of winds

what more shall I say of a feast of the senses
since I stood on Earth a hundred thousand years ago
all passing-present in the flash-by of a minute

I have paused to die with the sun and be born with the sun

my bones have known rocks' hardness, the wind's caress

I have drunk the flavours of Earth, I have bitten the fruits . . .

and just for a second, for all the family
I give thanks for a human life, for the human life

if we are free

In Ashdown Forest
August 23rd 2021

In Ashdown Forest, two days after the centenary of the first birthday of Christopher Robin Milne, at which he was presented with a certain Bear. The house where this happened is nearby and I can see the Poohsticks Bridge and some of the legendary stories almost taking place in the Hundred Acre Wood. I am here by coincidence, I hasten to add: I arranged the visit with no thought of the Milne connection or knowledge of the anniversary, but merely to meet a friend in a nearby village. Yet informed by the friend of the one and by the 'Times' of the other, and venturing upon the scene, I find myself taken back into my own childhood as far as I can go.

There are two or three fluffy animal-toys. Next is a large humming-top. Then I think books took over. The animal-toys – I have no idea of what genus but a bear does not come to mind – are the earliest things I remember. What are these companions? Do dolls (for that is what they are) assist the first steps to independence, with their tangible contours of identity? Is there a kind of infantile taking-charge? Or are they simply the first and only friends over whom we get our way, call all the shots? Whatever their first cause so to speak, what is remarkable is their sheer presence, as well in so many cases as their staying-power.

One of my children had to have to hand both Sam Teddy and Lamb Teddy (don't ask, I can't remember). Fortunately for his exhausted parents that didn't last too long. On the other hand my fifteen-year-old grand-daughter, one of the most sensible people I've known, still likes to know where Eddy (the teddy) is, if not quite as attached as she used to be. He must be all of thirteen or fourteen years old. Maybe it's that he doesn't change. Certainly Winnie-the-Pooh and his friends don't.

I relate to the Bear of Very Little Brain, to whom hums (verses, songs, poems) happen to come along. But even more to the donkey Eeyore, whose lugubrious remarks simply set the bar for umbrage, as if it were a herb he personally fed on. So here I am in a land of make-believe, than which nothing could be more real in the afternoon sunlight. Always the two worlds; and always, too, the glimpse of a smattering of contentment, however long ago it was that we abandoned our first creature comforts.

The human dimension
August 26th 2021

A final voice from a classroom of the past. Fifteen or sixteen years old, fifty-three years ago, lost like all the others, but as with a number of them, present to me in my own unseen movement between the rungs of time. In two poems Karen Briggs moves – for no more than a moment yet it stays – from child to adult; and for a moment too as I write I see what I have taken from a lifetime of teaching. Change has me on board. I have been refreshed.

In a word-work of art a change in perception is always on the cards. Hidden till the end or near it, at the same time concealed and revealed, in some way finally it takes over; and an aesthetic sense is harmonised and a mystery lingers. The economy of a poem takes us perhaps as close as we may come to what change can mean in the human dimension. Here two pieces individually and (fortuitously) together show us, in a simple but touching way, what art can get up to.

She was just a person at school. I was surprised when a report came round about her: all her teachers had to comment and virtually everyone saw no more than a silly creature. I had been aware of a quiet person with a certain sureness; and may have seen no more than that but for what she wrote.

THE FOUR-STROKE CYCLE

Why does this feeling suddenly sink into my soul?
Why am I sad?
I sit and look at the ceiling.
   'Today we'll go over the four-stroke engine.'
The voice drones on.
Suddenly I think, People are dying in Viet Nam.'

Why do I think of these things?
I must concentrate: Intake, compression . . .

Soon the yellow rose will bloom.
What's wrong with me?
I feel unhappy, I can't talk to anyone;
That's it! I want to communicate!
To be free! I don't care about the four-stroke engine!
I just want someone to say,
'What do you think?' and mean it.
'Intake, compression, ignition, exhaust.'
I am listening now, trying to learn;
But somewhere inside me I can't help thinking,
'Intake, depression, rejection, death.'

I AM

I have loved as no man has loved.
I have felt as no man has felt;
I have life and I give life.
I am life.

I was born and I have borne.
I will die and I am death.

I hold within me the thin
   gold-thread that is life.
I can make or break.

I am thistledown as it glides
   across the wind,
I am the devil rolling potatoes
   down a hill.

I have given and I must give
All that is in me:
Such is my lot.

I was created,
I have created.
I am hated and I am loved.
   I am needed.

   I am woman.

Kali
August 29th 2021

As a people we make Gods, and they can inform the person. They can unite us with Nature or with one another. They can remind us of the current of being, that is also of non-being. To know of them, as of some kind of living presence, is to take part in the role-play of the species.

Kali is Woman in her absolute power. She speaks for Life with all the force of Death and Night. Her *puja* or festival is often a fairly minor affair but in the year she is immediate, timeless, present, more so perhaps than any other deity. She is often portrayed with her foot on the body of her husband Shiva. In a terrible dance of triumph and anger after killing two universe-threatening demons she was herself endangering the foundations of all. Shiva lay in front of her and as she stepped on his body the horror of defiling it with her foot brought her to an awareness of what she was doing, and she was able to stop. Shown thus her tongue is extended, in recognition of the violation, it is thought. She is worshipped at midnight before the new moon, sometimes by dacoits (violent thugs, criminals). Often black or dark blue, with a garland of skulls, she is said not to give what is expected. She is at the heart of the person who walks with death to be reborn or of the universe that has again and again been consumed in fire. Since touched by that influence I have been glad to acknowledge what of woman I have within. It is the women of the world who are uncompromising in the battle for renewal. In spite of the skulls, the extended tongue (which I think of as a sign of strength), and the terrible anger, and maybe because of them, Kali is Woman in her true grace.

It is a paradox that I have not come to terms with that the three senior Hindu deities, Brahma, Vishnu and Shiva, are all male, and yet the female divine character is as vivid and free as they. Kali, Durga and Parvati are all wives of Shiva and in a sense all one, revealing as it might be said different aspects of womanhood. Durga in her way is all womanhood (and girlhood too), but primarily mother and death-defying protectress, carrying the responsibility of love. Parvati is Shiva's wife of the mountains, perhaps more lovely in a feminine way than her sister-selves. One may have an intimation of her in the hills, her light step unseen. As Durga the female divine is inexpressibly dear; as Parvati she is delightful. As Kali she is deeply necessary.

Kali
September 2nd 2021

(continued) It is how women are known to men that has posed such a barrier to their freedom. Rabindranath Tagore (see pages 140-149) at the end of a sonnet on 'Woman' sums it up: 'Man decorates you, veils you, makes you shy, / till you are precious, hidden, rarefied. / All lit up by his longing, his elation, / you are half woman, half imagination.' Tagore is as empathetic in his poems, novels and short stories to the nuances of the female character as any male writer; and his women are passionate, torn by circumstance – rather than lit up by an aggressive element. But he knew it had the right to exist. In a school he founded in Santiniketan in 1901 he ran into a storm of complaints from parents and others when he encouraged girl pupils to take up boxing; and had to abandon what was for the time and place a remarkable idea.

It may be worth tackling the question head-on. Is it the case that, as long as children are borne by women and not hatched in the laboratory, a level playing-surface for the sexes is as distant as being able to roll a huge boulder uphill? On the one hand, in the animal world to conceive, carry and bear a child is an expression of the greatest power there is. On the other, in the human world it narrows the options. I think in fact there is a great movement afoot to right the situation, insofar as it can be righted; but that a culture is still some way off where women are allowed the space not only to be as angry but to show their anger as liberally as men.

I have a daughter in her thirties and two grand-daughters in their teens. I would not want the Kali force to be lacking in their lives. It could be instrumental at key moments in clearing a path for themselves or others. Women's anger is needed to shock the world; and in its turn may come a tremendous contribution that men simply cannot make, quickened as it will be by a comparative lack of self-centredness. A great tide of creative thinking and practical solutions is at hand. Some think that the human destiny is a cyborg one, to become half machine. I think before that there is time for the female half of the planet to take the lead, but unlike the males in their time, without insisting on their dominance as if it were a right delivered at birth.

It is time for the daughters of Kali.

Chas
September 5th 2021

'I wonder in whose arms you are tonight
I wonder does he think he's doing alright
I don't really care but still I wonder
Just how long he takes to see the light . . . '

Chas Hodges (1943-2018) was a flaming comet in the murky heaven of the popular music world. Amongst a vast stream of inflated personalities parading various forms of addiction and excess, of imitation-American and imitation-rapture and tippy-tap imitations of everyday experience, he roared through. He himself sang in an American accent early on but took the decision to revert to his London roots, and with Dave Peacock in the duo Chas 'n' Dave left a trail of wonder. Their songs of London life and family goings-on and simple matters of the heart have always knocked me out.

Chas was the stand-out singer and instrumentalist: his piano virtuosity was concert-hall standard without the class of classical music, and a sight to behold. I went to three or four Chas 'n' Dave concerts and the glorious numbers they belted out, at times raucous, at times plaintive, at times just off-at-a-tangent delightful, whirl and dance in the memory. I wrote a school song once to the melody of 'London Girls', but never revealed the origin.

'Some people sing about Deutchy girls and girls from California
They might be alright for a night alright but don't trust them I warn yer
I've been to the east and I've been out west and I've been all the world around
But I aint seen none come anywhere near the girls from London town
Give me a London girl every time . . . '

His was a male voice in the tradition of Johnny Cash and Roy Orbison, an unaffected pre-Beatles letting-rip refreshingly free of the faint touch of whine that came in with the unisex 'sixties and has never quite gone. But he could be sentimental. 'Wish I could write a love-song' and 'Aint no pleasing you' blatantly play on the heart-strings; while 'Poor old Mr Woogie' is a fake dirge for the departed second half of the title of a genre. 'The Sideboard Song' is a mad dash, 'That's what I like' a celebration of clichés that has its own truth, 'Ponder's End Allotment Club' a simple tribute to a community. Chas loved growing vegetables; through the mad whirl of a star's life his feet were on the ground. There was no need to parade an identity. While the Beatles started a fashion for a version of youthful normality that touched the musical world like a blight, Chas 'n' Dave and their drummer Mick Burt shrugged free of all that. They simply were who they were, street-peddlers of blinding harmonies. What a record (so to speak) to leave behind.

One could mention so many other tracks on it: 'Gertcha', 'Down to Margate', 'That old piano' . . . but what comes over me now is the memory of a surprisingly small man, given his stage presence, whose hand I once shook seeing him outside a venue before a concert. (I can tell myself I have not lived in vain.) He played his voice like a wind-instrument maestro, he played the piano like a demon, he simply *was*.

That's what I like.

'The Power and the Glory'
September 8th 2021

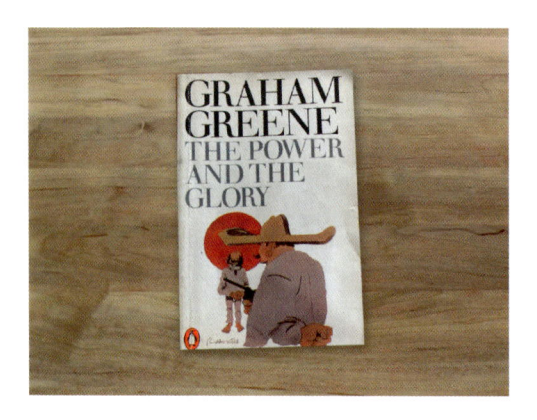

It is one of the great Christian works of art. After about fifty years I have re-read Graham Greene's novel about a Catholic priest in Mexico in the 1930s when the Church was outlawed and priests were shot. It is superb, more than an eye-opener, a revelatory insight into the cause and course of a good life. An act of faith absolutely lies at the back of such. A glimmer of the miraculous too, in the gift of transubstantiation, illuminates the story. I do not share that belief, and yet at a very far remove I do, in going forward along the line of existence. Where has that come from?

Greene has an antihero whose awareness of his feeble inadequacy fills the pages, and yet disappears before the reader's own perception of something other. A miserable creature, given to drink and the father of a child, he has the courage of someone without an ego. Not only does he know what matters, he is unable to help touching others with that knowledge; and yet his own crawling insect of a life is ever-present. What an achievement, for a writer in his early thirties, to find a perspective for human weakness, to make a saint out of a sinner, but with no displacement of the usual disqualifications for the holy or heroic. Human weakness is a part of human strength. The ambience of place, too, is quite remarkable in this novel. Yet even to use the word 'novel' diminishes it slightly. It's a statement of truth that cannot be arrived at without a fiction.

I have other favourites among Greene's oeuvre, notably 'Brighton Rock' and 'Our Man in Havana', but this plodding weary account of a journey, now read again so long later, leaves them in the shade. Where are the modern novels to approach this tawdry vision, this clenched fist that hides and protects a jewel, this open surrender? 'La Peste' or 'The Plague' by Camus comes to mind. But it's scarcely modern. So much of art aims so much lower than it used to. But really it's the surrounding noise, the critical acclaim that makes so much of it, that causes the problem. The lone adventurer is deterred, the different path abandoned, and we all make for the low ground. Yet while the classics remain there will be grounds for hope.

Re-reading this classic has reminded me of something. The Christian story which was a part of the background of my youth, and is (to a considerable degree) a part of the background of my country, has something tender to offer. Though I accept none of its apparatus I accept its existence, and more than I had realised, I think I accept its core. Which in some way (as probably with all religion) is to do with the kind of journey in this book. To be in a church is familiar to me; in old age I may let some of my childhood back in. For now I shall allow myself the occasional thought of Greene's whisky priest on his mule, and of one or two people I have known . . .

The ad fad
September 9th 2021

I get tetchier about ads as the years go by. A crashing sea of meaningless disinformation, with any amount of subliminal rolls and twists, even as one imagines oneself unaffected. The science behind it is always being developed, of how to catch people off balance, when they think they have their feet on the ground. I don't know if a grab can be subtle, but a good ad is a masterly attention-grabber. Literally diverting it captures, so to speak, the direction of your eyes. To think about the increase in the general barrage can be alarming. And yet if I see it as a genre of entertainment, then I simply remember my two favourite ads, irritation turns to admiration, and all's well with the world.

They are no more than packet-fronts, both from my childhood and both still going strong. One is all about strength and there's a slightly startling story attached to it. The Scott's Porage Oats shot-putter recently found himself with a new look, more Rudolph Valentino than John Wayne, and suddenly one is aware of a brooding poseur with an almost visibly muscular right thigh. It's a scream. Where's the cheerful guy gone who just picked the thing up and was about to throw it? Fortunately he seems to have returned and now both are available on the shelves. The other packet hosts the immortal Kellogg's Cornflakes cockerel. The story there's a lovely one. In the 1920s the Welsh harpist Nancy Richardson visited the Kellogg's factory in the USA. She played the harp to the nine hundred women who worked there and after a time they started to hum along. The event is said to have lasted all night. In the morning at breakfast William Kellogg said they were looking for a Cornflakes brand image and she suggested a cockerel for which the Welsh is *ceiliog* (with a hard c). So it ended up, in the colours of the Welsh national flag, for a good old rousing start to the day.

I liked my cereals and I liked their pictures. It's still a link back. I also liked a roadside ad for Guinness:

Toucans in their nest agree
Guinness is good for you.
Just try one today and see
What one or toucan do.

I was maybe ten years old and appreciated the picture and pun. Television was in its infancy then but now of course on-screen advertising is endless. Yet it too can be a winner. In India there was a marvellous series featuring a young boy and his pug. It laboured up steps behind him, it joined him in musical chairs, in a magic show, in a football game, in being at one with the trees and fields . . . but most enchantingly in my view when the poor lad had to sit for an important family photograph. There he is, scrubbed and serious, and suddenly a look of delight comes over his face as his faithful friend waddles up to him. Hutch Cellular Services were onto something there.

My view is that the ad fad is with us, it's addictive, it's invasive, it may be a sight more dangerous than it looks. The more innocent we can keep it the better – and that may well hold for its products too. After all, isn't the whole idea to appeal to the child in us all?

A vote of thanks
September 10th 2021

I seem to have given up cycling. Perhaps if I live in a less crowded area I shall get back in the saddle, but it's been a while now, and it feels of the past. And something in me wants to pay tribute to the partnership with a machine, to the simple act of moving about with such ease.

As a child I was allowed to drift about the lanes of Buckinghamshire on my own for hours. The only rule was that I had to be back by dark. Those afternoons now nestle in a companionable oneness with the world around, it seems. Memory has them as a time on my own when I was happy enough with life, or it with me, and no more was needed. Later, at about sixteen, I turned into a bit of a speed merchant at times. Once caught in a violent storm I could only think of lightning attracted to the bike's metal and with no cover to be had scorched along for miles. It was still a way of getting away from it all. One summer holiday with a basic mileometer clacking away I notched up an average of ten miles a day for the six weeks off school. Of course it wasn't all downhill so to speak. The best snack I've ever had was a packet of crisps – with the old blue twist of salt – after labouring up a mighty slope at Wanlockhead in Scotland. The bike was an ally in childhood, no doubt. But there were some good times with it later.

Apart from its mere use as a vehicle, as when for some months I went the few miles to work on it and back (there were of course a handful of different machines over the years), there were still times in adult life when it sang freedom. One was when I cycled to Hay-on-Wye in Wales from London to savour the second-hand book capital. But primarily in later years a couple of cycling trips with my younger son, each of a few days, brought back that spindrift ease and the sense, almost, of a mechanical symbiosis, that made the business of getting about such a pleasure. Which was increased of course by seeing him experience the same in his way. There was a hill in Bath up to the Youth Hostel that I simply walked up, wheeling my bike, while he could go no faster on his but stayed riding till the top. It was a good way to spend time together, away from the walls of the house and with life on the move, within the changing roads.

Perhaps the deeper tribute I want to pay is not to the bicycle but to the body, that machine we are so much one with, and that I cannot help but give up on at some not too far point in the future, or it on me. But let it be the bike for now that I say so long to and salute. What a neat invention it is. Not the modern electric version, not the motorised hybrid – but the bike itself. That's the thing.

Mare noctis
September 11ᵗʰ 2021

The sea of night. Night and the sea. I am blind, blind. It runs right through me, leaving me timeless, leaving me spaceless, leaving me nothing but a container of a wild current. Sea and the night pound in my bones. All of it, all of it comes down to this. My breath of a body is no more than a scoop, a second's container of a dark current. It seeps and swirls, it rocks and rakes, my outside is scattered, but something still holds it, I am back together, that is the way of it

blind, blind
listening, listening

a matchstick man new-formed and clinging to a shred of time

above him the stars, around him the night

within him the sea

again the pounding, the current unlocking, and then – out of that – there is a survival

in the sea of night for the breath of a second I have been connected to the earliest being and the newest direction and the last going

seeking, seeking
listening, listening
speaking, speaking

I am blind but awake

Finale
September 12th 2021

It's been a journey. A century of blog-observations, and each typed into a laptop the other side of a window from a close friend. What a companion to have by one, to oversee things with absolutely no interference, yet with a quiet expression of a natural tolerance, every step of the way. There is an expectation in those leaves of life, more life; and in a rugged casing of trunk and branches, I feel as though in myself a strength that stands or falls. The elm I wrote of in the first entry is with me and of me at the end.

People are suddenly discovering things about trees. Their communication with one another for the common benefit is startling, but only in terms of our previous ignorance. Any species of plant or animal is not so much a linked collection of individuals as an individual with many brains. One day the ridiculous human race will find out more about this. For now we make do with platitudes. Meanwhile Nature shelters and sustains us; and if we indulge a closeness that is there to be felt in terms that express closeness to ourselves, that is not in itself inapt. If we have an imagination there has to be room for a little make-believe. So way back I wrote a poem of the tree and myself called *The Brothers*; and so I return to an ally now, at the end of a journey, to record a companionship.

It's been a light road, a road of turnings, and of many views. I hope that anyone who travels it finds the occasional place to stop and rest for a moment, even if there are some to skip by. And there's an elm in leaf for a companionable end.